I RESPOND,
THOUGH I SHALL
BE CHANGED

I Respond Though I Shall Be Changed
Essays on the Thought of Eugen Rosenstock-Huessy

Copyright © 2023 by Peter J. Leithart

Theopolis Books
An imprint of Athanasius Press
715 Cypress Street
West Monroe, Louisiana, 71291
athanasiuspress.org | (318) 323-3061

Cover design and typesetting: Rachel Rosales

ISBN: 978-1-957726-12-0

Printed in the United States of America.

I RESPOND, THOUGH I SHALL BE CHANGED

ESSAYS ON THE THOUGHT OF
EUGEN ROSENSTOCK-HUESSY

PETER J. LEITHART

TABLE OF CONTENTS

ACKNOWLEDGMENTS

Several of the essays in this volume were previously published in books or journals. I am grateful to the original publishers for permission to reprint.

The "Introduction" was first published as "The Relevance of Eugen Rosenstock-Huessy" at FirstThings.com, on June 28, 2007. Used with permission.

"The Cross of Eugen Rosenstock-Huessy" was published in installments on my personal blog during 2017.

"Grammar on the Cross" first appeared in Wayne Cristaudo and Francis Huessy, eds., *The Cross and the Star: The Post-Nietzschean Christian and Jewish Thought of Eugen Rosenstock-Huessy and Franz Rosenzweig* (Cambridge: Cambridge Scholars Press, 2009), 225-242. Used with permission.

"The Social Articulation of Time in Eugen Rosen-stock-Huessy" first appeared in *Modern Theology* 26.2 (2010): 197-219.

"Stasis and Eruption: Eugen Rosenstock-Huessy as a Philosopher of 'Event'" first appeared in *Culture, Theory and Critique* 56.1 (2015): 59-72. Used with permission.

PREFACE

I've read, written about, and effused over Eugen Rosenstock-Huessy for three decades.

As far as I can recall, I first encountered his name in a footnote reference to *Out of Revolution* buried in one of R. J. Rushdoony's books.[1] I devoted more attention to Rosenstock-Huessy in the 1990s when Rev. Richard Bledsoe began citing him regularly at Biblical Horizons conferences. Merging Rosenstock-Huessy time-thinking with Jim Jordan's biblical theology proved an intoxicating mix.[2]

Researching for my doctoral thesis, I pored over Rosenstock-Huessy's books and essays on language to un-

---

1. Rushdoony's footnotes were my first introduction to many, many thinkers.

2. Rosenstock-Huessy lurks behind much of what Jim wrote during the 1990s and after. His most Rosenstockian books are *Crisis, Opportunity, and the Christian Future* (Monroe, Louisiana: Athanasius Press, 2016) and *From Bread To Wine* (West Monroe, Louisiana: Athanasius Press, 2020).

scramble some perennial puzzles concerning symbols, signs, rites, and sacraments. My first published reference to Rosenstock-Huessy (I think) was in a 1995 *First Things* essay, "The Politics of Emma's Hand," where I illustrated Rosenstockian grammatical sociology from observation of our second daughter, Emma Christine.

The papers collected here were written between 2007 and 2017, the fruit of an occasional elective I taught on Rosenstock-Huessy at New St. Andrews College in Moscow, Idaho. As I prepared lectures, I blogged quotations, notes, and summaries, which linked me to the small but dedicated community of Rosenstock-Huessy disciples—Norman Fiering, Wayne Cristaudo, Francis and Ray Huessy, Darrol Bryant, Michael Gormann-Thelen, and others. Those internet connections led to invitations to submit lectures and give papers, and, meanwhile, I published essays encouraging theologians to take Rosenstock-Huessy seriously. From those seeds these essays have sprung.

Only minor adjustments have been made to the original papers. Zach Parker of Athanasius Press made the citation form consistent throughout, changed references to "this paper" and "this article" to "this chapter," regularized capitalizations, and ensured ERH is always identified as Rosenstock-Huessy rather than Rosenstock.[3] Nearly iden-

---

3. Rosenstock is a family name. As per Swiss tradition, he added his Swiss wife's name "Huessy" when he got married.

tical paragraphs appear in a couple of essays; I let them be, so as not to disturb the original text and also because it afforded me the opportunity to use the Wodehousian term "snoot" more than once.

When I first conceived this collection, it didn't occur to me that 2023 marks the fiftieth anniversary of Rosenstock-Huessy's death. They have been years of obscurity and anonymity. Given his feel for history, Rosenstock-Huessy would have been neither surprised nor demoralized by his fate. As I write in the Introduction:

> "A seed must fall into the ground and die," Jesus said, "if it will bear fruit." Rosenstock-Huessy believed that this described a universal principle of history: Human beings bear fruit only in dying, and creative speech bears fruit only after germinating in the ground for a time. He would not be surprised that his work has been laid in an unmarked grave. But he doubtless died in hope that the stone would someday be removed.

I'm grateful to have a small part in opening his tomb.

Beth-Elim
Gardendale, Alabama
Trinity Season 2023

INTRODUCTION

"Obscure" hardly begins to describe the obscurity of the German-American thinker Eugen Rosenstock-Huessy (1888-1973). Though never a household name, he was admired during his lifetime by W.H. Auden, who wrote a foreword to one of Rosenstock-Huessy's books; Lewis Mumford; Harvey Cox; and Walter Ong. Before he left Germany in 1933, his intellectual circle included such prominent Jewish thinkers as Martin Buber and Franz Rosenzweig; Karl Barth was part of the so-called Patmos Group, of which Rosenstock-Huessy was a prominent member.

Since his death, Rosenstock-Huessy has all but vanished from public discussion. His historical studies inspired legal historian Harold Berman and historian Page Smith, but otherwise his work has left little mark on contemporary thought. A devoutly Christian writer, Rosenstock-Huessy is ignored by theologians, while Buber has remained well-known and Rosenzweig is enjoying something of a Renaissance.

Yet, Rosenstock-Huessy's work has never been more at home that it should be today. He anticipated a number of postmodern developments. In an essay "The Metabolism of Science," he deconstructs a book title, a set of lab notes, and Faraday's notebooks with the serious glee we have come to associate with Derrida. He said "Farewell to Descartes" long before Descartes-bashing became the popular sport it is today. Theologians who work, in Fergus Kerr's phrase, "after Wittgenstein," would find the *Sprachdenker* Rosenstock-Huessy a useful interlocutor, as would post-liberals who follow George Lindbeck's "cultural-linguistic" model of doctrine. Rosenstock-Huessy's historical work is attentive to culture, styles, fashions, festivities, calendars, and plays in ways that anticipate Robert Darnton, Natalie Zemon Davis, and Keith Thomas.

The scope of his life's work is impressively unclassifiable. He disdained the disciplinary confinements of the modern university, and the disdain shows. He wrote on language, religion and the Bible, calendars, time, and grammar. He published a massive history of the Western revolution and a three-volume *Soziologie*, as well as a monograph on his academic specialty—medieval German legal history. When he came to America, he took a chair in German language and culture at Harvard, but he could have taught sociology, law, philosophy, comparative religion, or any of a half dozen other disciplines. Harvard didn't know what to do with him. Since he talked a lot about God, they sent him to the divinity school.

It's not only the scope of his thought that impresses, but the integration. There is a passionate religious impulse behind everything he wrote, and it's all made immediately, existentially real. But he moves rapidly from the large movements of history down to individual and family experience. He writes in *Speech and Reality*:

> Whoever speaks believes in the unity of mankind. And he believes that the unity of mankind is not produced by physical or political or economic or racial reasons but by our faith in speech. We all believe in the Holy Ghost, the Oneness above and around our particular way of looking at the world. The individual's greatest freedom has as its corollary the spirit's greatest necessity. If all men are bound by one truth, then my-truth makes sense. If it does not, I go mad with my freedom.[1]

Leaving aside the question of what this means, or whether it's true, the mercurial movement of the passage is what first strikes the reader. Is this a statement about

---

1. Eugen Rosenstock-Huessy, *Speech and Reality* (Norwich, VT: Argo Books, 1970), 184.

the philosophy of language? Or politics? Or theology? Or psychology ("I go mad")? For Rosenstock-Huessy, it's all of these, but also none.

To take a more extended example: During the modern period, he writes in *The Christian Future* (1946), people believe that all large organizations are "rational, legal, and mechanical" as well as "logical and systematic." At the center of modern institutions, "there stands a typewriter" (a machine, and specifically a machine for generating plans and reports). Moderns are puzzled by the "perfectly unsystematic, irrational, antilogical" institution, "the poorest organization on earth" but yet "fully alive"—the family, which to the modern mentality seems a "colorful folly." At the center of the family is not a typewriter but "a bed and a stove"; the "unquenchable illogicality" of the family perturbs planners with a blueprint for the future.

The passion of the planners is commendable, but because their passion is right, their plans must be wrong, because their plans would eliminate passion. Life means vulnerability, the possibility of failures and wounds: "Unless [a man] is willing to call his wounds happiness, he must choose between living frailty and tin-canned orderliness." Rosenstock-Huessy often puts this in explicitly Christian terms: Life is always lived out on the cross, as we are stretched between the obligations of the past and the dreams of the future, between our own desires and the external world that confronts us. Like the family, the Church is a community that calls her wounds happiness, and this shows that she is alive. She is not a system, centered on a typewriter. At the center of the Church is an altar.

Systems may be eternal, but vulnerability is inherent in life: "He who lives can die. A 'system' which never lived may linger on forever." Rosenstock-Huessy is not merely talking about literal death. What distinguishes a living thing from a mechanism is that living things "slough off" the old stages and bring new ones. He points out that the word *existence* contains this notion of passage from one state to another; it "literally means a getting out of one form and into another." Everywhere "life is never contained in one form but in the slope from the old which is doomed to a new which triumphs over death." Children think life comes before death, but that's not true. Death—the death of man and wife to their own independent individuality precedes birth. Before a child is born, he says, the love of the parents comes "as the first signal of their individual transiency." When a woman and a man fall in love, they are both getting ready "to abandon ship" as individuals. Loves "allows them to make room for the best of their own body outside of themselves and beyond themselves." Two people who get married acknowledge they are mortal and "open an exit to life, beyond their two corpses."

In a philosophical climate where "bodiliness" and otherness are all the rage, Rosenstock-Huessy's theories of speech and his attention to somatic life are worthy of attention. In theological terms, he is a thoroughly anti-Gnostic thinker. The body leads the mind; events precede thoughts and reflections about events. Of all the parts of the body, Rosenstock-Huessy noted, the brain alone doesn't reproduce cells, making it the deadest organ of the body. The pragmatic thrust of his thought was also evident in his life. Early on, he was a prominent young German legal scholar, but he taught adults in church and community settings throughout his life, founded an industrial newspaper, and set up labor camps and Camp William James in order to bring intellectuals, farmers, and workers together in combining their energies to pursue a Jamesian vision of the "moral equivalent of war."

He is also a radically anti-rationalist thinker, but was equally hostile to ignorant hostility to science. Science, he says, is really good at studying dead things. Dead things are predictable, and you can do repeatable experiments. Living things are illogical, unsystematic, unpredictable, uncontrollable. Studying dead things is a useful endeavor, and it is one of the great achievements of the West to give space to a sub-community devoted to science and given the right to "systematic error." More broadly, he dismisses the rationalism of the Greeks and of the Enlightenment as an adolescent obsession:

Natural reason is a very special reason sprouting in the unfulfilled mentality between 14 and 25. It is the Reason of the classroom student. Greek philosophy, eighteenth century enlightenment, America common sense or pragmatism, are gigantic superstructures of these uprooted minds and unloved bodies in their in-between age.

Openly orthodox, Rosenstock-Huessy was also a remarkably progressive thinker, embodying what Chesterton, one of Rosenstock-Huessy's favorite authors, described as the adventure of orthodoxy. This is evident particularly in his meditations on time, and the fundamental temporal orientation of his work. He observed that institutions, ideas, and systems have their day and then something new is needed: "Philosophies have their time. It is a misunderstanding to attribute a perennial character to any particular philosophy. Philosophy is the expression of a zeitgeist. Philosophies must be buried at the right time. The Jesuits know that Thomism is dead." He spoke of the world entering a "Johannine" age of history, an age of the Spirit that would move quite differently from the earlier ages of the Church: "each generation has to act differently precisely in order to represent the same thing. Only so can each become a full partner in the process of Making Man."

The progressive remaking of the human race is central to Rosenstock-Huessy's understanding of Christianity. In *The Christian Future*, he discusses the "resurrection of the body" in the context of the work of the Spirit, the third article of the creed. In the beginning, God made man in his image, and this means that the whole history is a "process of making Man like God." The new thing in Jesus' resurrection and the gift of the Spirit of resurrection is that Christ "enables us to participate consciously in this man-making process and to study its laws." Following patristic sources, Rosenstock-Huessy calls this "anthropurgy," comparing the extraction of pure metal from ore with the process of purging the dross to purify and renew humanity.

One of the laws of anthropurgy is the resurrection of the body. For Rosenstock-Huessy, resurrection is about reproduction. Resurrection means not only that new kinds of human beings are made but that they can be reproduced:

> A new soul, a fresh originality of the human heart, thereby survives the man or nation in which it came to birth and incarnates itself in a spiritual succession of typical representatives through the ages. For there are definite new phases of human existence never lived before . . . and, if they are genuine, they force themselves upon man's plasticity with such impressiveness that they don the bodies of later men and women in turn, and shame them into the same time.

Luther was an original, the first of a new type of man, but soon there are thousands of "Lutherans." And they really are *Lutherans*, little Luthers, stamped with the image of their leader!

This is not reincarnation, nor mere repetition of the earlier form of man. Rosenstock-Huessy uses St. Paul's image of a "natural" seed that rises as a spiritual body to describe how a "new human type" arises when one seed of a new humanity is planted. His own example is St. Francis. Though Francis had no natural children, "Franciscan humanity has flourished ever since, and not only in his Order. The Franciscan way of life, immortally portrayed in *The Imitation of Christ*, became daily bread for the lives of countless Christians of all denominations, even the most radical Protestants." This even has political import, as the Franciscan way of life spread to the royal houses of Europe—he mentions the Habsburgs—and to America. Abraham Lincoln entering conquered Richmond in 1865 on foot without entourage is the political triumph of Franciscan mentality. Ruler and servant become one.

Rosenstock-Huessy also develops a kind of Trinitarian historiography and anthropology. He links the articles of the creed—which moves from Father, Son, to Spirit— with three millennia of church history. During the first millennium, the Church was concerned with being body of Christ (Son); the second concentrated on restoring creation to its Creator, since after men restored to God, they could begin to purge the world of ungodliness (Father); the next millennium will be the age of the Spirit, which will concentrate on "revealing God in society" (Spirit).

Trinitarian patterns also shaped the development of Western individualism. He points out that the original meanings of the word *individuum* is "what cannot be subdivided" and is specifically used of the Trinity. Peace treaties from 800 to 1815 were concluded *in nominee individuae Trinitatis*. Applied to human existence, the word meant that the "individual" was made in the image of the *individua trinitas*:

> Man, between 1500 and 1900, could be called an *individuum* because he participated both in God's qualities and in the world's qualities as well. In the middle between the atom and the Trinity, he boasted of "individuality." This *individuum* of the Renaissance boasted loudly in the fact of the whole world: "I am unbreakable! I am impregnable!" And Renaissance Man intimidated the powers that be so that they honored his divine triune likeness to the *Individua Trinitas*!

As a result, "Genius has been given his berth, through patents, copyrights and many other individualistic laws"; and as the image of the Trinity, he "cannot move in any one field without moving at the same time in all others. If our mode of prayer changes, our modes of thinking cannot help changing also."

Rosenstock-Huessy is worth reading for how he writes. He interacts very little with other scholars, and this makes him look *sui generis*, which in some respects he certainly is. But he also claims that he virtually memorized Chesterton's *Heretics* and *Orthodoxy*, and his exposure to Chesterton is evident in the sharp and witty aphorisms that punctuate his work:

> We ourselves never ignite the light of reason; it is kindled in us.

> Things are predictable because they do not speak. He who speaks is unpredictable.

> Only the word makes what has happened into history.

> Without speech man would have no time, but merely be immersed in time. Animals are time's toys. Men conquered time when they began to speak."

> "God's mind is just as much a metaphor as His elbow. Our mind is not nearer to God than our body."

"Modesty is the veil under which life can change."

"What we know of ourselves is what is dead in us."

"The future does not consist of the extension of existing trends, nor of ideological opposition to them. The future must be created."

Rosenstock-Huessy is intriguingly paradoxical, counterintuitive, often apparently and flagrantly wrong-headed. On the one hand, he's a profoundly Christian thinker. He says that the cross is at the center of human history, and he develops his entire view of human experience, history, society, and speech around the notion of a "Cross of Reality," which describes human life stretched in agony between past and future, inside and outside. He links this universal cross with the specific event of Jesus' death on the cross, arguing that Jesus makes a permanent difference in history.

Yet he also says things that few Christian thinkers would dare to utter. Such as: "the power to speak is God because it unites us with all men and makes us the judges of the whole world." And "polytheism is a thousand times truer than deism or atheism." Near the end of *Out of Revolution* (1938), he suggests an addition to the creation of Adam in the Sistine Chapel:

We might conceive of a pendant to this picture; the end of creation, in which all the spirits that had accompanied the Creator should have left him and descended to man, keeping, strengthening, enlarging his being into the divine. In this picture God would be alone, while Adam would have all the *Elohim* around him as his companions.

Against the near-universal conflation of biblical and Platonic motifs in Western theology, he seems to favor the gods of Homer:

Plato's ideas are abstract gods. Philosophy is reduced and therefore neutralized truth from Parmenides to Hegel. Only the whole of language together is true. But the Greeks began to say: "Being" and "I am that I am" (which is not in the Bible, but in its Greek translation), and there the academic world of ideals began. "I am" together with "I was not" is meaningful. But "I am that I am" is idiocy.

Rosenstock-Huessy would not be surprised that his work has fallen into comparative obscurity. "A seed must fall into the ground and die," Jesus said, "if it will bear fruit." Rosenstock-Huessy believed that this described a universal principle of history: Human beings bear fruit only in dying, and creative speech bears fruit only after germinating in the ground for a time. He would not be surprised that his work has been laid in an unmarked grave. But he doubtless died in hope that the stone would some-day be removed.

CHAPTER ONE

THE SOUL OF EUGEN ROSENSTOCK-HUESSY

When I published some articles on the German-American philosopher Eugen Rosenstock-Huessy (1888-1973) on the web a decade or more ago, I received an email from Norman Fiering, Director and Librarian Emeritus of the John Carter Brown Library at Brown University. A student of Rosenstock-Huessy's at Dartmouth College during the 1950s, Fiering has been President of the Eugen Rosenstock-Huessy Fund, which maintains Rosenstock-Huessy's work in print and promotes the study of his work.

Being in Rosenstock-Huessy's classroom must have been an overwhelming experience. After a long and productive academic career in an Ivy League university surrounded by the best of the best, Fiering still feels the force of his undergraduate teacher. Rosenstock-Huessy was prodigiously learned, as is evident from his wide-ranging published work on philosophy, political and legal history, sociology, the four Gospels, theology, modern science, and, above all, speech. He would arrive in class with a three by five note card, and lecture for an hour and a half from those few jotted reminders. It was not, however, Rosenstock-Huessy's learning alone that left a lasting impression. Still today, Fiering describes himself as being under Rosenstock-Huessy's "spell," and reminisces about moments during lectures when his teacher seemed to come under the inspiration of some higher power, seemed to "take off." Many have compared Rosenstock-Huessy to an Old Testament prophet in an effort to capture the reality of a man who, in Fiering's words, served as a "vessel of the spirit."

You can hear something of his power as a teacher in the nearly 400 hours of lectures taped by students at Dartmouth between 1949 and 1957, available at the Rosenstock-Huessy Fund website.[1] He is not a sensitive teacher. A Jew converted to Christianity in his teens, he berates his comparative religion students for their ignorance of the

---

1. https://www.erhfund.org/

Christian creed and their easy relativism in matters of religion, lashing them with a vigor that would today provoke student protests if not lawsuits. His lectures seem to meander, from ancient religion to suburban life to courtship to education to politics to personal anecdotes, but there is method in the meandering, as Rosenstock-Huessy demonstrates the existential and social centrality of religion to his skeptical and blissfully uncommitted students.

At one point in a lecture on comparative religion, he mentions Jesus' warning about pearls and swine, quipping "All education is throwing fake pearls before real swine." That comment is not isolated, and the disdain for the protocols and deadening specializations of modern academic life it expresses is one reason for the obscurity of Rosenstock-Huessy's work since his death in 1973. Though never a household name, Rosenstock-Huessy was admired during his lifetime by W. H. Auden, who wrote a foreword to one of Rosenstock-Huessy's books, Lewis Mumford, Harvey Cox, Walter Ong, and Reinhold Niebuhr. Before he left Germany in 1933, his intellectual circle included prominent Jewish thinkers like Martin Buber and Franz Rosenzweig, and Karl Barth was part of the so-called "Patmos Group" of which Rosenstock-Huessy was a prominent member.

Others in his circle have continued to rise in reputation. Barth is well established as the greatest Protestant theologian of the last century, Buber has never left the public eye, and Rosenzweig's work is enjoying a posthumous revival among both Jewish and Christian thinkers, cited regularly by the mysterious *Asia Times Online* columnist who writes under the pseudonym "Spengler." Yet, Rosenstock-Huessy remains virtually unknown. His historical studies inspired legal historian Harold Berman and prolific American historian Page Smith, but otherwise he has left little mark on contemporary thought. Much of his work remains untranslated into English, and what is available in English is published by the obscure Argo Books of Norwich, Vermont.

In an article on the triangle of Rosenstock-Huessy, his wife Magrit (known as "Gritli"), and Rosenzweig, Michael Zank describes Rosenstock-Huessy as being "by academic standards an oddball." Were he alive, Rosenstock-Huessy might be happy to return the insult, but he would first acknowledge its truth. *I Am an Impure Thinker* is the title of one collection of his essays, and he wears the epithet proudly. But his impure oddness is not a pose; it is deliberate, and deeply rooted. One way to get at Rosenstock-Huessy's oddity, as a man and a thinker, is to say that he was a man of "soul." He does not speak, teach, or write for fame, money, or to impress. As he says in a chapter on Descartes in his magisterial *Out of Revolution* (1938), "I am hurt, swayed, shaken, elated, disillusioned, shocked, comforted, and I have to transmit my mental experiences lest I die. . . . By writing a book, a man frees his mind from an overwhelming impression." He speaks, teaches, and writes for survival, because life presses speech from him as an outpouring of his soul. Understanding what that means takes us to the heart of Rosenstock-Huessy's work.

Jesus told His disciples to "take up the cross and follow Me," but Rosenstock-Huessy claims that the cross is not peculiarly Christian but universally human. Every human being lives at the center of what he describes as the "Cross of Reality." The horizontal axis of the cross is a temporal axis, stretched between the past and the future. The present time is always a complex combination of past and future, and the conflicting and equally legitimate demands of tradition and innovation create tensions, strife, and pain. The vertical axis of the Cross of Reality is a spatial axis. Contrary to Cartesian or Newtonian conceptions, space is not "pure extension" or an empty vacuum, but dual, divided between the space of my inner life and the space of the world outside. Socially, too, space is divided between one's in-group and all out-groups. Like the temporal axis, the spatial axis brings conflicting yet legitimate demands. I must be loyal to my in-group, but I have equally pressing obligations toward those outside. Trying to meet these obligations wounds us and tears us in two. To live is to be rent in four directions, by the past and the future, by the inside and the outside.

It's possible to relieve the tension and pain of life by amputating one or the other pole of the Cross. We can renounce the future and enclose ourselves, as the Amish do in central Pennsylvania, in a safe cocoon of the past, or we can renounce the past with revolutionary violence. Torn by the cross, we can find a counterfeit unity in commitment to fascist politics. We can create impermeable walls around our community to keep all outside influences at bay, or we can attempt to live wholly on the "outside" as rootless cosmopolitans without *any* "inner" group. These are all infantile efforts at "adjustment," and impossible in any case. Try as we might, we cannot escape the detritus of the past or the relentless pressure toward the future; especially in an age of global electronic communication, we cannot find a protected inner space nor eliminate the effects of family, our first in-group. Acting on the temptation to come down from the cross can only produce deformities in human society and the human psyche. To live well, to live maturely and *humanly*, we must first accept that life is life on the cross.

Rosenstock-Huessy's life-long obsession with speech becomes clearer within this account of human experience. Speech is our primary means for living out this cruciform existence and integrating its multiform demands. Through the speech of teaching, the past is relayed to a new generation, which is in turn called to listen in order to create a human future. At the same time, the old must also listen to the yet-inarticulate shouts of the young, lest the next generation be dominated exclusively by the spirit of sons and not by the double spirit of fathers and sons. From within our in-group, we must speak to those outside, in hopes that they will come to understand our language, and if we are to escape war, our inner group must be willing to listen to and learn from those outside our walls.

Time is as much an obsession for Rosenstock-Huessy as speech. He challenges the modern tendency to flatten time into a mechanical "ticking of the clock," urging instead that time is multi-dimensional. The regimented time of a factory and its shifts is not the same as the lyrical time of contemplating a sunset or the play-time of sports. Nor is time merely a uniform passage of moments. Time is articulated into units, what Rosenstock-Huessy calls "bodies of time," by human action and speech. This is an important aspect of the temporal axis of the Cross of Reality. Living wisely in time means knowing when a trend or habit of the past has become decadent and needs to be buried so that a new thing can begin. *We* create the fissure between past and future by declaring that something is over and done. Peace treaties put war into the past and initiate a future of peace, while fashion designers, moviemakers, and marketers increase sales by dividing the time of style into "old-fashioned" and "fresh." At a broader level, history has seams, moments when one epoch is brought to a close and a new epoch initiated.

Against this background, we can understand what Rosenstock-Huessy means by "soul." Soul is not, he insists against some philosophers, identical with the mind. Mind is inherently conservative, oriented to the past pole of the Cross of Reality. The brain, Rosenstock-Huessy likes to point out, is the sole organ in the human body that does not reproduce cells. He also appeals to the experience of adolescence to show that the mind is not the leader of the body but frequently its lowly servant. A young man surging with hormones is not driven by *thoughts* of sex. His *body* is in charge. Thought assists the young man's agitated body by giving him schemes and plots to fulfill his desires.

Soul is not mind also because, for Rosenstock, the mind is timeless while the soul is thoroughly embedded in time. Contrary to much of the Christian tradition, and particularly to popular piety, Rosenstock-Huessy insists that the soul is not fuzzily "supernatural." The term "soul" applies to "everything about men and women that has to do with the total duration and unity of their existence," including "destiny, profession, marriage, children, honor, fame, disappointment, suffering, sacrifice, personal names." Soul contrasts not only with mind, but with body and spirit. Bodily needs arise and are met within a brief span of life. We get hungry, and relieve our hunger by working so that we can buy food. Desire masters us, and we relieve ourselves in sexual encounters. These bodily needs, even when we fulfill them repeatedly over a lifetime, do not constitute a unified life-story: "No matter how many daily wages are added together, they will not equal the course of a life; no matter how many sexual acts, they will not equal a marriage."

Concerns of the "spirit," by contrast, "go above and beyond the time limits of souls." Spirit unites souls together, whether in space or time. Spirit is what unites fathers to sons, and what unites my family to another: "We should understand all matters of the spirit as an inherited succession of souls." Spirit is a "structure that reaches out" beyond the individual, to which an individual must yield if his life is going to transcend the material demands of the body. Spirit can grip a single person, but it does so "only in order to reach others through him."

Body and spirit differ in their time-spans. Bodily time-spans are short, and the time-spans of the spirit are inter-generational, and ultimately, in Rosenstock-Huessy's Christian framework, the time-span of *the* Spirit stretches from creation to eschaton, forming human history into a single story. Soul is in between, uniting the time-span of the individual life. The Spirit is changeless, working to unite changing humanity and a changing world. But the soul that responds to the Spirit "must remain open to change. Obedience to the appeals of the spirit is the life of the soul."

On Rosenstock-Huessy's account, then, it is clear that "soul" is not "Ego." Soul is inherently responsive, not the self-standing "I" of Descartes. Souls don't exist in an empty landscape, but are formed in encounters with others. Souls are called forth by names, and the life of the soul has a grammatical structure. Souls are awakened first by being addressed from the outside, in the second person, as a "thou." Only over time do souls come to speak of themselves in the first person. In the world of human souls the grammatical first person is not first in human development. Psychologically and socially, the first person is the grammatical second, the "you" addressed from the moment of birth when parents say, "You are John" or "You are Mary." To be a soul is to say, in Rosenstock-Huessy's counter-Cartesian formula, *respondeo, etsi mutabor*—"I respond, although I shall be changed."

Speech shapes the soul, and the soul also comes to expression in speech. For Rosenstock-Huessy, the speech of the soul is not idle chit-chat or detached speculation. Speech is proclamation, command, memory, song, poetry, self-committing oaths in which the speaker is accountable for his utterance. In part, these forms of speech are squeezed out by life on the Cross, as the pressures of the Cross force speech from our souls, lest the Cross tear us apart. In part, these forms of speech are the soul's means for achieving integrated life when all the forces of the world are tearing it in shreds. We speak in response in the agony of our suffering in order to find common life with other souls, in order to cast a line in hope to the future and to the outside.

Above all, the soul is the human capacity to survive death. A soul is born in being named and addressed, but takes shape and comes to fruition in the experience of suffering on the Cross of Reality. A soul, Rosenstock-Huessy says, "is born through the growing pains of suffering in action." The soul is that in human beings which enables us to suffer the partial deaths inherent in life, and to rise again to a new future. Soul enables the single man to die to singleness and be reborn as a husband; it's the power Father Zossima talks of that enables a woman to lose a child and yet love the remaining children; it's the power that makes it possible for a student to leave playtime behind and enter the world of work and politics; it's what makes it possible for a woman to retire from active life without bitterness or desperation. The Christian soul in particular is the soul that believes the Christian gospel, which announces that the deaths of the Cross are always gateways to new life. As it knits together the deaths and rebirths that constitute a life, soul molds what could be a fragmented life into a unified body of time.

In this last sense particularly, Rosenstock-Huessy is a man of soul, for his life was marked by periodic deaths and resurrections. As a young man, he was a rising academic star prior to World War I, but initially refused to return to academic life after the war. In a letter written in 1946, he describes the post-war German university as a place of dead works, and says that returning to academic would have been a sin against the Holy Spirit. Instead, he took a position with Daimler-Benz as editor of a company newspaper, which led to a life-long interest in industry and labor.

When Hitler was elected, Rosenstock-Huessy discerned the direction of German culture and politics, and in 1933 he left Germany for the United States, where he lived the rest of his life. His life is thus divided into epochs, bound together by his faith that each death would beget new life.

By the same token, Rosenstock-Huessy would not be surprised that his work has fallen into comparative obscurity. "A seed must fall into the ground and die," Jesus said, "if it will bear fruit." Rosenstock-Huessy believed that this described a universal principle of history: Human beings bear fruit only in dying, and creative speech bears fruit only after germinating in the ground for a time. He would not be surprised that his work has been laid in an unmarked grave. But he doubtless died in hope that the stone would someday be removed.

Rosenstock-Huessy's work has never found a more welcome intellectual environment than it does today. He anticipated a number of "postmodern" developments. Already in the middle of the twentieth century, he was predicting that the world was entering a paradoxical age of simultaneous globalization and re-tribalization. In an essay on "The Metabolism of Science," he deconstructs a book title, a set of lab notes, and Faraday's notebooks with the serious glee of a Teutonic Derrida. He said "Farewell to Descartes" long before Descartes-bashing became the popular sport it is today. Theologians who work, in Fergus Kerr's phrase, "after Wittgenstein," would find the *Sprachdenker*

Rosenstock-Huessy a useful interlocutor, as would post-liberals who follow George Lindbeck's "cultural-linguistic" model of doctrine. Rosenstock-Huessy's historical work is attentive to culture, styles, fashions, festivities, calendars, play, in ways that anticipate Robert Darnton, John Bossy, Natalie Zemon Davis, and Keith Thomas.

In the 1960s the American church historian Martin Marty said something along the lines of "Rosenstock-Huessy was ahead of his time. He still is." That same judgment applies forty years on. But perhaps, finally, we are coming close to catching up, and perhaps his work is ready to overcome not only the author's death but to come from the shadowy valley of academic indifference. Perhaps Rosenstock-Huessy will finally prove to be the man of soul that his former students have long recognized him to be.

As a man of soul, however, Rosenstock-Huessy would not want his work to be offered as another set of theoretical proposals. He spoke from the center of the Cross, spoke with all the uncanny power of a man acquainted with death and new life, spoke in hope that his words would awaken other souls. His voluminous writings will have the effect he wanted only if they inspire singing and dancing, commands and attentive listening, courageous action and exultant praise.

CHAPTER TWO

THE CROSS OF EUGEN ROSENSTOCK-HUESSY

Theologians ignore the work of Eugen Rosenstock-Huessy (1888-1973). My purpose is to show why that is a mistake.

Rosenstock-Huessy was not always as obscure as he is now. After emigrating from Germany to the United States from Germany in 1933, he taught at Harvard and Dartmouth, and his books received admiring notices from W. H. Auden, Martin Buber, Harvey Cox, Lewis Mumford, Walter Ong, and others. Rosenstock-Huessy influenced the work of legal historian Harold Berman and historian

Page Smith,[1] but his writings seem to have left little mark elsewhere. Other members of the German "Patmos Circle," particularly Franz Rosenzweig and Martin Buber, have retained a presence in current discussions, counted worthy to be placed in conversation with Levinas, Heidegger, and other postmodern luminaries. Rosenstock-Huessy remains in obscurity.

Rosenzweig especially, a personal friend and erstwhile disciple of Rosenstock-Huessy's, is enjoying a revival. A number of recent collections of Rosenzweig's writings are available, there is a recent edition of Nahum Glatzer's book-length life-and-thought volume, and a number of books and articles on his work have recently been published.[2] Buber's work has never left the public eye. By con-

---

1. In the Acknowledgments appended to his magisterial *Law and Revolution: The Formation of the Western Legal Tradition* (Cambridge, Mass: Harvard University Press, 1983), Berman says that he began writing the book when he went to study legal history at the London School of Economics, having gone to London "under the inspiration of Eugen Rosenstock-Huessy, to study the impact of the English Revolution of 1640-1689 on the development of English Law," and he adds that his work builds on Rosenstock-Huessy, as well as on the work of R. H. Tawney and T. F. T. Plucknett. Rosenstock-Huessy is cited regularly throughout Berman's book.

2. The University of Wisconsin Press released a new translation of Rosenzweig's *Star of Redemption* in 2005, translated by Barbara Galli. In addition, see Franz Rosenzweig, *Philosophical and Theological Writings* (Paul W. Franks and Michael L. Morgan, trans.; Hackett Publishing, 2000); Barbara Galli, ed., *Cultural Writings of Franz*

trast, Rosenstock-Huessy's work is maintained in print in English by the obscure Argo Books of Norwich, Vermont, which distributes some of his shorter works in photocopied form, with the occasional hand-written correction. Neither a biography[3] nor any thorough synthesis of his thought

---

Rosenzweig (Library of Jewish Philosophy; Syracuse University Press, 2000); Randi Rashkover, *Revelation and Theopolitics: Barth, Rosenzweig and the Politics of Praise* (London: T&T Clark, 2005); Robert Gibbs, *Correlations in Rosenzweig and Levinas* (Princeton: Princeton University Press, 1992); Nahum Glatzer, *Franz Rosenzweig: His Life and Thought,* 3rd ed. (Hackett Publishing, 1998). Over the last decade or so, a number of articles have explored aspects of Rosenzweig's thought: Zachary Braitermen, "'Into Life'??! Franz Rosenzweig and the Figure of Death," *AJS Review* 23:2 (1998), 203-21; Leora Blatnitzky, "Dialogue as Judgment, not Mutual Affirmation: A New Look at Franz Rosenzweig's Dialogic Philosophy," *Journal of Religion* 79:4 (1999), 523-44; Barbara Galli, "Franz Rosenzweig and the name of God," *Modern Judaism* 14:1 (1994), 63-86. Rosenzweig is seen as a suitable interlocutor with Heidegger in Peter Eli Gordon, "Rosenzweig and Heidegger: Translation, Ontology, and the Anxiety of Affiliation," *New German Critique* 77 (1999), 113-148; Steven Kepnes, "Rosenzweig's Liturgical Reasoning as Response to Augustine's Temporal Aporias," in Randi Rashkover and C. C. Pecknold, eds., *Liturgy, Time, and the Politics of Redemption* (Radical Traditions; Grand Rapids: Eerdmans, 2006).

3. The most complete biography I have located is in Harold Stahmer's introduction to Rosenstock-Huessy's *The Christian Future: Or, The Modern Mind Outrun* (New York: Harper Torchbooks, 1966), vii-lv. An interview and a letter are included in *I Am An Impure Thinker* (Norwich, VT: Argo Books, 1970), 166-190. See also http://www.valley.net/~transnat/erhbio.html and http://www.argobooks.org/biography.html.

has ever been written.[4] George Allen Morgan wrote a helpful summary of Rosenstock-Huessy's "Christian linguistic
social philosophy"[5] in 1987 (now twenty years old), but
when the collection of aphorisms is eliminated, Morgan's
book is only seventy-six pages long, with chapters of sometimes only two pages.[6] The bibliography appended to Morgan's book (compiled by Lise van der Molen) reveals that
much of Rosenstock-Huessy's work remains untranslated
into English. Few articles have been devoted to Rosenstock-Huessy during the past several decades, and even

---

4. See M. Darrol Bryant and Hans R. Huessy, eds., *Eugen Rosenstock-Huessy: Studies in His Life and Thought* (Edwin Mellen Press,
1986). Rosenstock-Huessy has fared a bit better in Europe. A number
of works have been translated into Dutch, Portuguese, French, and
Russian, and several are available in fairly recent German editions:
Der Alter der Kirche (with Joseph Wittig; Verlag Klaus Boer, 1996);
*Heilkraft und Wahrheit: Konkordanz der Politischen und Komischen
Zeit* (Brendow Verlag, 1991); *Soziologie: Im Kreuz der Wirklichkeit* (3
vols; Talheimer Verlag, 1997). Even in German, a number of Rosenstock-Huessy's books are available only in reprint editions. There is no
collected works, nor any critical editions.

5. Morgan, *Speech and Society: The Christian Linguistic Social Philosophy of Eugen Rosenstock-Huessy* (Gainesville: University of Florida
Press, 1987).

6. Remarkably, given the importance of Jesus and the notion of a
"Christian Era" in Rosenstock-Huessy's thought, Morgan gives only
a two-page chapter to "Jesus Christ: The Center of History" (ch. 12)
and another two-pager to "The Christian Era" (ch. 13). Much of
Morgan's book, further, consists of quotations, without much interaction, analysis or criticism.

those that deal with him directly are usually more directly concerned with Rosenzweig.[7] When I searched for theological articles on his work, the yield was even slimmer.[8]

This neglect of Rosenstock-Huessy is not altogether surprising. A self-professed "impure thinker,"[9] his thought is as unsystematic as it is wide-ranging. Known, if he is known at all, as a *Sprachdenker*, he was originally trained as a legal historian and taught medieval legal history. He wrote a massive history of Western civilization,[10] specu-

---

7. The only article I found from the last two decades that names Rosenstock-Huessy in its title is Harold M. Stahmer, "'Speech-Letters' and 'Speech-Thinking': Franz Rosenzweig and Eugen Rosenstock-Huessy," *Modern Judaism* 4:1 (1984), 57-81. A number of articles from the 1940s are available through JSTOR, but they are few and far between.

8. An ATLA search uncovered only one article on Rosenstock-Huessy published over the last decade: Elfriede Buchsel, "Das verlassiche Wort: Eugen Rosenstock-Huessy und Johann Georg Hamann," *Neue Zeitschrift fur systematische Theologie und Religionsphilosophie* 42:1 (2000), 32-42.

9. The initial essay on Descartes in *I Am An Impure Thinker* includes this typical passage: "I am an impure thinker. I am hurt, swayed, shaken, elated, disillusioned, shocked, comforted, and I have to transmit my mental experiences lest I die. And although I may die. To write a book is no luxury. It is a means of survival. By writing a book, a man frees his mind from an overwhelming impression" (2).

10. Eugen Rosenstock-Huessy, *Out of Revolution: The Autobiography of Western Man* (London: Jarrolds Publishers, 1938).

lated on the future shape of Christianity,[11] formulated a grammatically-based sociological theory,[12] and examined the gospels as the fulfillment of ancient forms of speech and culture.[13] His published correspondence with Rosenzweig remains one of the important documents of modern Christian-Jewish relations.[14] He scorned academic jargon and style, making no friends with his observation that the impersonal style of modern scholarship manifests the same impulse toward abstraction that came to political expression in the trenches of World War I.[15] He rarely interacted with contemporary scholars, rarely provided a genealogy of his own thinking, rarely attempted to answer questions that others were asking. He wrote punchy, aphoristic prose that sometimes verges toward poetry.

He was literally, and deliberately, unclassifiable. Like others of the Patmos circle, he resisted disciplinary confinements of the modern university. He was such a devout and vocal Christian, and referred to God so frequently in class,

---

11. *Christian Future.*

12. Eugen Rosenstock-Huessy, *The Multiformity of Man* (Norwich, VT: Argo Books, 1973); *The Origin of Speech* (Norwich, VT: Argo Books, 1981); *Speech and Reality* (Norwich, VT: Argo Books, 1970).

13. *The Fruit of Our Lips* (Eugene, OR: Wipf & Stock, 2021).

14. Eugen Rosenstock-Huessy, ed., *Judaism Despite Christianity* (University of Alabama Press, 1969).

15. *Out of Revolution*, 3-15.

that Harvard dispatched him to the divinity school, where folks get paid for their Godtalk. But he never claimed to be a theologian and disdained much modern theology. Perhaps more importantly, Rosenstock-Huessy's work is not entirely that of a "thinker"; there is a pragmatist strain in his work that prohibits him from isolating thought from action. After serving in the German army in World War I, though already established as a rising scholar, he turned down offers from universities, the German government, and religious editors to take a job with Daimler-Benz, where he edited a company newspaper. Throughout his life, he was involved in student camps, worker camps, and adult education in various civic and church venues.

For all the difficulty of encompassing his work, Rosenstock-Huessy's work deserves to be more widely known and more deeply studied, particularly by theologians. Rosenstock-Huessy's themes resonate with contemporary movements in theology, from Lindbeck's post-liberal "cultural-linguistic" notion of doctrine to the contemporary emphasis on praxis, from the Radical Orthodoxy's insistence on the inescapability of theology to the recovery of patristic hermeneutics. Before there was "narrative theology," he was arguing that theology must narrate and preach rather than analyze. Long before the recent revival of interest in Hamann, Rosenstock-Huessy was hailed as the new

"Magus of the North."[16] Before "otherness" became a buzz-word, he had placed responsiveness to the voice of another at the heart of his thought. Before theologians began their assault on Descartes, he had replaced the Cartesian *cogito* with his own motto: *Respondeo, etsi mutabor*. He anticipates a number of postmodern themes, particularly in his studies of speech, his observations on body and temporality,[17] and his hostility to modern disciplinary boundaries and the modern policing of religion. It seems a propitious time to give some renewed attention to this intriguing writer.

I. Once–for–all

Rosenstock-Huessy would not be surprised that his work has fallen into comparative obscurity. "A seed must fall into the ground and die," Jesus said, "if it will bear fruit." Rosenstock-Huessy believed that this described a universal principle of history: Men bear fruit only in dying, and creative speech bears fruit only after germinating in the ground for

---

16. *Christian Future*, ix. He was given this title in 1959 upon receiving an honorary doctorate from Munster.

17. This is wonderfully summarized by his comment that modern thought has seduced us to think that God is closer to our minds than to our bodies: "But the mind of God is as much a metaphor as his elbow. Our mind is not nearer to God than our bodies. Yet this division of the world into a physical and mental has blinded many as though the mind were more divine than our kidneys" ("The Metabolism of Science," 4, in *Rosenstock-Huessy Papers, Volume I* (Norwich, VT: Argo Books, 1981).

a time. Christian living, he emphasized, was a participation in the unique event of Jesus' death and resurrection, and this means that Christian living is a series of crucifixions and risings. He would not be surprised that his work has been laid in an unmarked grave. But he doubtless died in hope that the stone would someday be removed.

This brings us to the central concern of this paper, the meaning of the cross in the work of Rosenstock-Huessy. "The Crucifixion is the fountainhead of all my values," he wrote, "the great divide whence flow the processes most real in my inner life, and my primary response to our tradition is one of gratitude to the source of my own frame of reference in everyday life." He immediately goes on to add that "our chronology of B.C. and A.D. makes sense to me. Something new came into being then, not a man as part of the world but The Man who gives meaning to the world, to heaven and hell, bodies and spirits." A bride who receives her husband's name is set in a "new realm" and all her actions are "credited" to that realm. Similarly, "in His name we [as His bride] enter a realm of freedom unknown to mere heirs."[18]

This is classic Rosenstock-Huessyism. He cites the historical event of the crucifixion, and immediately turns existential, describing how the cross sets the frame of reference for his own experience. In the next sentence he has moved

---

18. *Christian Future*, 102. Hereafter cited as *CF*.

from inner life to the crux of history, endorsing the division of time between B.C. and A.D. Also characteristically, he employs a marital image to describe the historical change that comes with Christ, and, obsessed as he is by speech, he cannot stop himself from inserting something about new names.

The following treatment of his cruciform philosophy is organized around the several insights contained in this quotation: First, I examine what Rosenstock-Huessy says about the uniqueness of the cross. Second, I explore the existential dimension of the cross, the way it serves as the source for all the real processes of "my inner life" and the "frame of reference in everyday life." Third, I look at how Rosenstock-Huessy describes the effect of Jesus' cross and resurrection on the history of human civilization. Throughout, we will find that the cross has two intertwined significances for Rosenstock-Huessy. He sees the single historical event of the crucifixion of Jesus as central to all human history, but he also claims that human life in general is lived out on what he calls the "Cross of Reality," which becomes not only a key to personal experience but functions as a anthropological and social paradigm. In the last section the essay, I turn my attention specifically to this aspect of Rosenstock-Huessy's cruciform thought.

First, the cross as a once-for-all event. In *The Christian Future*, Rosenstock-Huessy talks about the divinity of Christ, but frames this creedal dogma within a discussion of once-for-all events in history: "Every value in human history is first set on high by one single event which lends its name and gives meaning to later events."[19] Crusades are cheaply bought now, but they are all the fruit of an original first crusade; first Francis, and then a Franciscan way of life; first Luther, and then a host of Lutherans. The meaning of crusading is established as a reality by the first crusade: "The one unique event must precede the many."[20] The definite article precedes the indefinite, and makes the indefinite possible.

The united complex event of Jesus' cross-and-resurrection is the once-for-all event of all once-for-all events, and the possibility of recurring deaths and resurrections in individual life and in civilization depends on Jesus' work: "crucifixion (or last judgment) and resurrection would not be known as everyday occurrences in our lives if they had not happened once for all, with terrific majesty."[21] Jesus plants the seed of death-and-resurrection, and this bears fruit repeatedly in moments of transforming anguish.[22]

---

19. *CF*, 103.

20. *CF*, 103.

21. *CF*, 103-104.

22. Rosenstock-Huessy explains his parenthetical reference to the last judgment in a footnote: "In the Crucifixion, with the accompanying darkness, rending of the curtain in the Temple, etc., that which is to happen finally has happened once already; and for the faithful the second coming of Christ as Judge really began with his first coming.

As the Crucified and Risen Man, Jesus creates a new form of humanity, a new style of human being. He is not thus merely a man among men, but "the norm, the way, the truth, and the life to be developed by us beyond the state in which we find ourselves." He is "my maker" because He is the first man "who was neither Greek nor Jew nor Scythe, but complete and perfect humanity, and each of the rest of us, if we are not simply jealous like Nietzsche, must be content with being his men."[23] We cannot judge and measure him without making him simply "a" man. On the contrary, "he is the measure by which we must judge ourselves; his life gives meaning to ours; and, to sustain the stage of human perfection which he achieved, the word 'man' would have been quite inadequate."[24] Rosenstock-Huessy implies by this that Jesus is insurmountable. We might attempt to leave what he calls the "Christian era" or reject the gospel, but Jesus made such a difference in history that no one, not even the most hostile enemy of Christ, not even Anti-Christ, can escape being Christ's.

The Crucifixion judges us all, because we know that we would have behaved like Pilate or Gamaliel or Peter or Judas or the soldiers. The Last Judgment will make known publicly what those who have died with their First Brother already experience daily, that our Maker remains our Judge" (*CF*, 103n6).

23. *CF*, 104.

24. *CF*, 104.

II. The Cross in Christian Experience

But what does this mean? How is the cross and resurrection reproduced in human life since the cross and resurrection? Essentially, Jesus incorporated death into life. Christian faith means faith in a God who makes death into a *positive* feature in life.

Rosenstock-Huessy observes that human life is suffering, battle, pain, shock, failure, elation. Human beings are always torn, always riven. That is true of human beings since the dawn of creation, and Rosenstock-Huessy's observation of this fact is not particularly original or insightful. But Rosenstock-Huessy sees much of human life, individually and collectively, as an effort to deal with suffering and death. By being the first Man, Jesus establishes the possibility of a different stance toward suffering and death. Life after the cross, and life in the light of the cross, is a life in which death never has the final word, but where death is the means and path toward new, more expansive life. He testifies that this is the story of his own experience. Writing in 1946, Rosenstock-Huessy says, "twenty years ago I felt that I was undergoing a real crucifixion. I was deprived of all my powers, virtually paralyzed, yet I came back to life again, a changed man. What saved me was that I could look back to the supreme event of Jesus' life and recognize my small eclipse in his great suffering. That enabled me to wait in complete faith for resurrection to follow crucifixion in my own experience. Ever since then it has seemed foolish to doubt the historical reality of the original Crucifixion and Resurrection."[25] This is not a matter of "survival." It is renewal through death, an experience of death as a "positive feature" of life, the key to abundant life.

Another way to say this is that Jesus reveals the "Living God." Unlike the gods of the philosophers, the Living God is never an object. He is not examined or measured by us, but examines us with his eyes before we open our eyes or mouths. This living God confronts us in the midst of life, not at the level of reason: "The living God cannot be met on the level of natural reason because by definition he crosses our path in the midst of life, long after we have tried to think the world into a system."[26] God is always revealed in the cross; God always comes first of all in the form of catastrophe, raising the possibility of death: "That power which compels us to answer a question of life and death—and 'any part of the world, sun, earthquake, crisis, revolution, can become a god when we feel that it is a power urging this question upon us'—is always our God; 'the power which makes the atheist fight for atheism is his God.'"[27] The questions God or the gods put to us need not be verbal, but when they confront us they "demand our devotion, not lip service." A person can be wholly godless

---

25. *CF*, 102.

26. *CF*, 96.

27. *CF*, 96.

only if he acknowledges no power at all above him; a godless person would have to "be all of god himself." Modern man is not godless but polytheistic, pursuing many gods or "values"—Rosenstock-Huessy names "art, science, sex, greed, socialism, speed—these gods of our age devour the lives of their worshipers completely."[28] Powerfully addictive though they are, none of these gods can finally satisfy, nor can they enslave forever. Promiscuity wears thin, "socialism annoys the man of sixty," and "greed is hardly conceivable to a young person." These gods fade, but the Living God is the God of the future and so always endures.[29] Faith in the God of the future, who is also the God revealed in the cross, enables us to die to the gods and move toward the future. Without the revelation of the cross, death to the gods would be impossible: The impotent man might as well commit suicide, since he has lost his reason for life. The revelation of the Living God enables us to slough off the gods when they grow old.

Gods can not only be shed, but this shedding process is the means of transformation. Because of Jesus, "death has paradoxically become the key to everlasting life." Christians can anticipate death in order to overcome it:

---

28. *CF*, 96.

29. *CF*, 97.

By learning to anticipate the inevitable end which the pagan fights off, man has robbed death of its paralyzing gloom. Anticipating the worst, he can bury his dead in time. A pagan was ready enough to die physically—for his family, temple, guild, nation, or race—but these he held to be immortal and therefore without flaw. He could not admit the necessity of letting them die when the time had come; hence all went down together.[30]

Through the cross, Christians recognize that life will necessarily involve occasional deaths to their old ideas, ideals, allegiances. Anticipating and embracing these partial deaths as the beginning of new life and new future, Christians are not faced with the threat of a total death as the pagan was. We know that various "gods" will come and go, and we can shed each without anxiety, because we know that there's renewal on the horizon.

When death is incorporated into life, and anticipated in faith, life becomes abundant. This was Jesus' purpose—not to negate life, but to give life, abundantly: "Christianity is not a decadent worship of death for its own sake, but the discovery that including death within life is the secret of the fullest life."[31] Monks and hermits witness to this: By

---

30. *CF*, 68.

31. *CF*, 124.

giving up the world before death, "they proved that death is an essential element of living, in fact its sharpest ingredient." There are other forms of anticipating death as well: "Any father, manager, or teacher has to practice resignation and let the young learn by doing things he could do better himself; for he knows that one day he must die and they must take his place." This is not from "our instinct of life" but "from our wisdom of death." For Rosenstock-Huessy this is what it means to have a soul: "Man as an animal organism lives forward from birth toward death, but, as a soul who knows beforehand that he will die, he molds his life looking backward from the end."[32]

What happens when we are torn, divided, riven without recognizing that it is a "human privilege," without faith in the resurrection? We lack soul, and we cannot live abundantly. There are also political and historical consequences. "If a man does not know that it is perfectly normal to be thus torn, and that a divine power exists which integrates persons by uniting them in communion, he will surrender to any man-made power that seems to promise unity, fixity, and security." This is, he says, one of the sources of the attraction to Nazism: "Torn men are dangerous men. They will go to hell and worship the devil of power for power's sake, in the form of any wild desire, unless we reestablish

---

32. *CF*, 124.

the power of the Spirit in its original white heat."[33] Efforts to avoid the cross, and the suffering that comes with it, condemn us to insignificance. "The basic law of all history: only where extreme resistance is overcome does a new origination become possible. Usually we live according to the law of least resistance."[34]

III. The Cross and civilization

Jesus not only establishes the possibility that individuals might live abundantly, but as *the* Crucified and Risen Man, he creates new possibilities for history, forms a new epoch of history, the Christian era, and forms the possibility of a new civilization. To understand fully what Rosenstock-Huessy means by this, we need to examine his sketch of ancient social forms.

In an Augustinian move, Rosenstock-Huessy argues that civilizations are formed according to the direction of their loves. Love is expressed in call and response, in speech and listening. We turn to listen to the one we love, and when a community turns to listen to the voice of the beloved, a civilization is born. The speaker can address from the past or future, from inside or outside, and as the appeal and speaker changes, as listeners turn to new lovers, a new civilization is born. Civilizations are also responses to

---

33. *CF*, 15.

34. Quoted in Morgan, *Speech and Society*, 105.

death. Throughout history, "God becomes known to us in all the powers which triumph over death."[35] All human civilization prior to Jesus organized itself as an effort to avoid death, or treated it as purely negative, yet in these attempts we can discern a "growing knowledge of God."[36]

Tribes are the first form of civilized human life. Tribes discerned god in the power that maintained a tribe in existence after its members died. For tribes "God is identified with the spirits of the tribe's ancestors," and tribes overcome death "by simple denial: the ancestors aren't 'really' dead, but have simply migrated to a happy hunting ground."[37] For the tribe, love is directed toward the ancestors, and the living direct their attention to the dead because "the dead look at the living," which, Rosenstock-Huessy says, is "the basic law of the tribal constitution." As Morgan says, the tribe is thus "dominated by the past. Everything is sacrificed for the past. The spirits of the ancestors govern. They are highly suspicious of youth and oppose all change." Future is "represented by the stone altar on which innovators are sacrificed—the widespread sacrifice of the firstborn child is an expression of this attitude."[38]

---

35. *CF*, 92.

36. *CF*, 93.

37. *CF*, 93.

38. Morgan, *Speech and Society*, 35-6. Rosenstock-Huessy lays this out in abbreviated form in *The Fruit of Our Lips*, 1-8.

Cosmic, or temple-building empires, come into being in a sudden shift from the tribe. Flood legends often describe a cataclysmic baptismal boundary between tribal past and imperial present. In pagan empires, God was known "as eternal cosmic order revealed by the stars and imitated by the stone walls and temples and pyramids built for worship." Temple civilizations do not overcome death by denial but by circumvention: "the sun-god and his temple enjoy deathless duration."[39] Imperial temple-building peoples attempt to "bypass" death by "climbing to the sky."[40] In tribes, the dead speak to the living, but in cosmic empires, the heavens speak to the earth. Heaven tells a tale of eternal recurrence: Sunrise and sunset follow one another each day, and the constellations move in recurring patterns. As a result, for cosmic empires, time is still: "There were no real endings or genuine beginnings, no novelty, no true future." Instead, the imperial civilization is "stunted into a kind of eternal present," emphasizing space instead of time and establishing "timeless" political systems.[41]

Israel introduced a new love, new time, a new speech, and hence a new civilization. Jews claimed that God was the power who created and who then "could enable His people to discount the passing of all visible things and wait

---

39. *CF*, 93.

40. Morgan, *Speech and Society*, 37.

41. Morgan, *Speech and Society*, 37-8.

for His future coming as Messiah." Death is not "denied or ignored," as in paganism, but for the Jews it has "only a negative significance. It is something to be endured." But it is endured in hope. Israel is oriented to the future. The Lover who speaks to Israel speaks from the end of time: "This is the new direction of its love—toward the one Living God, the ever-coming God." And this means that the mode of Israel's existence is oriented to the future, but it is oriented in patience, in anticipation and not in consummation. Abraham left his own land and waited for the fulfillment of God's promises, and this waiting-in-exile is a crucial contribution of Israel to ancient civilization.[42]

---

42. Morgan, *Speech and Society*, 39. Other shifts in civilization follow from this. Sabbath releases Israel from the domination of ancestral spirits to rest in God. Israel bestows dignity on the individual. Only tribal heroes, as spirits, can speak in the first person to the tribe; in Egypt, only gods could address Pharaoh as "thou." But Israel is a "we," a collective in which everyone can address and be addressed by others. Instead of the myth of recurring floods, as we find in other civilizations, the Bible teaches there is only one flood, which broke the imperial power once-for-all and revealed that "every act of the Living God is unique and unpredictable, like his subsequent rainbow." Even when Israel became a monarchy and a kind of empire, the prophet Nathan could correct the king; the census, an instrument of empire, was forbidden, and the Word of God was written down, making possible a flow of God's word into the future. Israel's temple was not a limited space that mirrored heaven; it did that, but it was also thought of as containing powers—the water of the sea—that would flow out universally and consecrate the world to God (39-40).

Finally, the Greeks created a "mixture of the tribal and imperial ways of life." In contrast to earlier civilizations, Greeks united not through exercise of political authority but by a spiritual kinship. Greeks were united by the sea, and the seaport was a place of entry for outsiders into each individual Greek city-state. Greeks could look at themselves from outside, through the eyes of strangers, as well as from within. Greek pluralism in myths and politics gave rise to a universal poetry that united Greeks (Homer, then the tragedians), and also to the universal thrust of philosophy. Greeks created "the life of the mind, of liberal arts and sciences inspired by the muses, the free realm of ideas, as a way of finding unity outside political pluralism." Achilles and Priam can recognize each other's humanity and claims, and the scene of their mutual tears is a sign of the greatness of Greek humanism. This presented also yet another way of evading death: So long as men remained spectators, they could forget that life depended on suffering and death.[43]

------

43. Morgan, *Speech and Society*, 42-43. The Greeks introduced the impersonal "it," viewing the world scientifically and philosophically. As Morgan says, "In place of the 'I' behind the tribal mask, the 'Thou' with which Pharaoh was embraced by the gods, and the 'we' of God's people, the humanist uses the third person 'it' to neutralize human history by speaking in generalities about 'a god,' 'a rite,' etc." Earlier civilizations had organized themselves in a particular mode of time—past, present, or future, but these seemed incompatible with one another, and necessarily in conflict. The Greeks "did the impossible" by forming "spare time, play time, leisure of a theater-going, school-attending, games-watching public." They gave the world the

How does Jesus affect this situation? In part, Jesus does for civilization what he does for individuals—he makes possible a *positive* stance toward death, and this produces a civilization that can shed the old with equanimity. At times, Rosenstock-Huessy says that Jesus unified all earlier civilization, all earlier human speech. Jesus was thus "the first to turn mankind's direction toward unity," and he did this by "placing himself at the source of the times, the heart point, from which we may come ever again to the formation of tribes, empires, humanists, and the true Israel." He made the "fullness of time" available by standing at the source point of all times.[44] At other times, he says that Jesus unified man specifically in bringing *time* into a unity. Each ancient civilization had grasped an aspect of human time, but could not bring the times into unity. What Jesus revealed is the fact that "humans can progress from fragmentariness to completeness only by the cross, only by surviving the death of old allegiances and beginning new ones."[45] This was the theme of His whole life. He lived under the law in order to do away with the law, to die to the law. His entire life was a matter of scouring away the old to make way for new. He refused "success" in his own life, giving Himself instead to the founding of the church, and

---

"free time" of art, science, and play (43).

44. Morgan, *Speech and Society*, 45.

45. Morgan, *Speech and Society*, 45.

through this "unsuccessful" career makes himself the most successful man in history.[46]

IV. Cross of Reality

Christianity's history is a constant penetration of the cross more and more deeply, and more and more broadly, into human experience and society. New epochs are made when the cross comes to mark a new "sphere of our minds or bodies."[47] In the new era that Rosenstock-Huessy saw coming, the cross needed to penetrate into social life. In preparation for this new epoch, it is necessary to reformulate Christianity's dogmas about the cross, translating it into "non-ecclesiastical, post-theological language" in an effort to show the pervasiveness of crucifixion. The "Cross of Reality" is a deliberate bid to formulate something like Bonhoeffer's religionless Christianity.

Rosenstock-Huessy uses the Cross of Reality to describe the suffering at the center of human experience, and the unsystematic and unsystematizable complexity of life.

---

46. Morgan, *Speech and Society*, 46. In *The Fruit of Our Lips*, Rosenstock-Huessy argues that each of the gospels shows Jesus taking up a past time and transforming it into something new, taking up a past form of speech and founding a new speech. All the old languages merged in Him, and came to new expression, a universal, Pentecostal expression that speaks to everyone. As he says, Jesus "saved the straying Gentiles and the locked-up Jews . . . by cross-fertilizing the four paths of speech."

47. *CF*, 165.

While philosophers and scientists, metaphysicians and physicists might describe the world as a system, actual reality and actually lived human life is a "perpetual suffering and wrestling with conflicting forces, paradoxes, contradictions within and without." Life stretches us in opposite directions, tears and rends us, yet through this tearing makes us new.[48] Specifically, human beings are stretched out on two axes. The horizontal axis is a temporal one, stretching between past and the future. The vertical axis is spatial, as we are stretched out between "inner" and "outer."

The difference between space and time, and the priority of time, are obsessions for Rosenstock-Huessy. Time is not, as mathematics depicts it, a straight line, since a line does not distinguish qualitatively between past and future and cannot capture the multiform shape of human time. Time is an undifferentiated line for animals, which know "no future but only perfect and imperfect tenses, only processes that have ended or processes still going on at any given moment."[49] For humans, a timeline is an illegitimate spatialization of time, and Rosenstock-Huessy insists that time and space are experientially quite different. Space is experienced "as a whole." Time, by contrast, comes to us as moments, fragments, as "a phantom moment or as innumerable phantom moments." Time becomes organized

---

48. *CF*, 166.

49. *CF*, 166.

and packaged into hours, days, years, epochs only "*because we say so.*" Times exist because "they are history-made units built by our faith, out of innumerable moments."[50] Time experienced this way is never uniformly one time: "*Nobody lives in one time.*"[51] The past and future always inhabit the present, and so human beings are always being pulled backward by the obligations imposed by the past and moving forward seduced by hopes from the future.

The spatial axis of the Cross of Reality is the axis that stretches us between "inner" and "outer." Individually, we all have an "inside" bounded by skin, and a world outside us. Corporately too, each community constitutes itself by setting a boundary between "insiders" and "outsiders." The social body too has its skin, and must protect itself against infection from outside.[52]

We hang at the center of this cross, nailed and pulled in all four directions at once: "man's life, social as well as individual, is lived at a crossroads between four 'fronts': *backward* toward the past, *forward* into the future, *inward* among ourselves, our feelings wishes and dreams, and *outward* against what we must fight or exploit or come to terms with or ignore." This is a painful position, often ag-

---

50. *CF*, 167.

51. *CF*, 167.

52. *CF*, 168. The analogies with Mary Douglas are quite pronounced here.

onizing, and so we are tempted to relieve the tension by embracing only one of the four points of this compass. But the goal of life is not "adjustment," as modern psychology might suggest; the goal is integrating the demands of each, all of which are legitimate demands.[53] Rosenstock-Huessy points out that "it is obviously fatal to fail on any front—to lose the past, to miss the future, to lack inner peace or outer efficiency." If we rush forward without acknowledging the past, "acquired qualities of character and civilization would vanish," but if we dwell in the past "we cease to have a future."[54] Integrating these demands is not easy, and we never

---

53. *CF*, 169.

54. *CF*, 168. In various lectures and other writings, Rosen-stock-Huessy suggests, for example, that the Athenian Academy or the medieval universities represent a presence of the outside on the inside. The university brings healthy tension into the city by being a center of universal thought in the midst of a particular, potentially parochial polis. Rosenstock-Huessy addresses the charge that the Cross of Reality, true as it may be, is trivial and obvious. Yet, he claims, "our 'natural' minds deny this trivial truth." We are inclined to deny that we "respect the past," and instead reduce the past to a "cause" of the present and future. This prevents us from seeing that, to use Augustinian terminology, we are always "distended" between memory and expectation. Further, we tend to forget that "all thought is an inner conversation of a fellowship, and all 'nature' external and outside the fellowship." Perhaps most importantly, the Cross of Reality exposes the fantasy of the philosophical stance of "onlooker," as if anyone could step outside the cross and observe himself hanging there (*CF*, 168n3). It is not trivial, further, because modern philosophy has operated with a simple duality of inner and outer, ignoring the other

fully achieve integration. Life is mobile, not static. We are tossed here and there, shocked by the demands thrust on us from the outside, surprised by the unanticipated future. While we strive for integration, we cannot be at every point of the cross equally at the same time. Life is thus "a perpetual decision." We must determine when to perpetuate or revive what is past, and when to let the past die and lie quietly buried. We must recognize the difference between those "within" our circle *to* whom we speak and the things "without" *about* which we speak. To live is to dance, as we preserve "a delicate mobile balance between forward and backward, inward and outward."[55]

Elsewhere, Rosenstock-Huessy treats the four points of the cross as four dimensions or aspects of time. Time has "four leanings, four inclinations." He labels these lyrical, analytical, dramatic, and epochal. Though different dimensions or experiences of time, these correspond to the space-

---

duality of past and future. To the subject/object distinction, Rosenstock-Huessy wants to add the temporal distinction of "traject" and "preject." As a "traject," man is carried along by the current in the old boat of stable culture; as a "preject," he must build a new boat when the old one loses its seaworthiness, and he must launch in a new direction when it's clear that there are impassable shoals ahead. Traject names man and society in their evolutionary context; preject names man as revolutionary. We are all trajects and prejects, and can be these simultaneously—as we, for example, might continue in a steady job (traject) when we get married (preject) (*I Am an Impure Thinker*, 8).

55. *CF*, 168.

time Cross. Lyrical time is "inner" time, when, singing or watching a sunset or absorbing ourselves in a book, we "are lost on the inside." Analytical time occurs when attention is focused outward. Lyrical time focuses on the *mood* of time and ignores time's movement, but analytical time ignores mood and is very conscious of the ticking clock. A factory manager attempting to organize his workers' time efficiently is in analytical time; a basketball player who keeps glancing at the shot clock is also experiencing time analytically. Dramatic time is oriented to the future. It marks a break in time, with the dramatic moment the fulcrum of the split between a before and an after. Dramatic time makes new time and creates future. Epochal time, finally, is oriented to the past. We experience time epochally when we focus on the repetitions and routines that persist from the past into the present. A sunset can be experienced as a moment of epochal time (it happens every evening) or as lyrical time (when we lose ourselves in the unique beauty of *this* sunset). Epochal time, like lyrical time, seems to stand still, not because we are lost inside but because nothing seems to change.[56]

---

56. This summary is taken from notes on transcribed lectures on the Cross of Reality, prepared by Richard Feringer, available at http:// www.argobooks.org/feringer-notes/r03.html, 2. The Cross is about the multiformity of man in another way as well. Man is body, mind, soul, and role. As body, he is outwardly directed; as mind, inwardly; as soul, he overcomes death to achieve a new future; in a social role as law-giver of ceremonial head, he maintains the traditions of the past.

Like individuals, societies are also on the Cross, and thus always threatened by internal division. Lawyers and teachers pull back as politicians push forward; poets rhapsodize on traditional landscapes while engineers cross the scenery with new bridges. Like individuals, societies are always in danger of lurching in one direction or another, but integrate the demands of the Cross by a division of labor, distributing responsibilities for past and future, preservation of the inside and mission to the outside, among various subgroups or individuals: "teaching, ceremony and ritual preserve our continuity with the past, and teachers, priests and lawyers serve on this front for all of us." The "inside" is built up by "playing, singing, talking together, sharing our moods and aspirations, and on this inner front poets, artists, and musicians are typical representatives." On the outer front, we aim to "control natural forces" and manipulate them "for our ends in farming, industry and war," aided by "scientists, engineers and soldiers." Finally, future is kept alive by "religious and political leaders, prophets and statesmen," whose task is to initiate change and pull

---

All are necessary: "You cannot live without all the time alternating between these four attitudes. There is no way out. You are always one or the other of these four" (Lecture notes, 9). Personal freedom exists in the matrix of these differing demands. Freedom is a relation to time, the ability to decide what is past and therefore should be surpassed, what is future (Lecture notes, 13).

us into the future.[57] Integration of these social demands requires that "specialists" make room for those leaning in the other directions, recognizing the legitimate claims of others without abandoning their own legitimate claims. Societies move through the tensions of the cross and are made new only through love, forbearance, and mutual honoring and recognition of differing gifts.

Rosenstock-Huessy's main argument in favor of the Cross is "the fertility of its applications,"[58] and to him the Cross is as fertile as weeds. It provides him with a ready-made inoculation against reductionisms of all sorts. Cruciformity implies the "multiformity" of man, society, history, human life. As an example of reductionism, Rosenstock-Huessy notes the work of Josiah Royce. While commending Royce's philosophy on loyalty, he criticizes the attempt to reduce every virtue to an expression of loyalty. Loyalty is oriented toward the past, and if loyalty is an absolute imperative, there is no place for the obligation to break away in a new direction. Loyalty must coexist with love, which stretches the person toward the future: "to say that a man leaves father and mother and cleaves to the wife of his choice out of loyalty simply does not make sense."[59] Scientific modernity in general is reductive

---

57. *CF*, 169.

58. *CF*, 168n3.

59. *CF*, 170.

in another direction, obsessed with the "outward front" as it treats everything as "something merely to classify, experiment with, describe, control." This is an essential pole of human existence, but you cannot treat your wife like that.[60] Intellectuals are prone toward reductionism as well. Thought, Rosenstock-Huessy argues, is "provoked by our ends," and particularly by the end of death. But thinkers would not have time to think death and the future unless other members of the society devoting themselves to other tasks, guarding other poles of the Cross of Reality. How can a philosopher dream his dream of reason unless he can sleep at night, unless he can be confident that the Gestapo is not going to beat his door down at any moment?[61]

The Cross of Reality also serves as an analysis of the social death that "lurks in wait for us on every front, if we fail." Death can occur when any one of the four poles is forgotten: "Decadence, for instance, means being unable to reach the future, in body, mind or soul."[62] Decadence is a failure to reach the future. Revolution, by contrast, is a failure in the direction of the past, anarchy a failure to build inner unity, and war a failure to engage peaceably with the external world. No community can be purely

---

60. *CF*, 170.

61. *CF*, 171.

62. *CF*, 173.

self-contained, and will collapse if it does not have some kind of contact with a larger world outside.[63]

Intellectually, the Cross of Reality transcends the division between philosophy and theology that came into existence in the middle ages. Philosophy has worked in a spatial framework, emphasizing "the world of space or the knowing mind and a corresponding logic of timeless abstractions." For philosophy, time appeared "foreshortened," and in the sciences to which philosophy gave birth the same spatialization is evident. Theology, by contrast, is interested in history—Adam, Abel, Abraham, Jesus and the Judgment. The "division of labor" between philosophy and theology was a "working compromise" between Christianity and Greek philosophy, but this compromise is no longer viable. The Cross of Reality attempts to "overcome the division and fuse space-thinkers and time-speakers into one new profession" that is no longer exactly philosophy nor exactly theology. This would "accomplish the penetration of the Cross into the last stronghold of paganism within our own traditions," the stronghold of philosophy and science.[64] The Cross even enables Rosenstock-Huessy to transcend the boundary between Christianity and other religions. As a Cross of *Reality*, the cross is not an exclusively Christian symbol: "the great civilizations of the Orient,

---

63. Morgan, *Speech and Society*, 6-7.

64. *CF*, 173-4.

China and India" are "under the Cross too." To illustrate, he integrates Buddha, Laotse, Abraham, and Jesus into a single unified, cruciform tension[65]: "The founders have mastered each direction of the Cross of Reality by living the pure eye, the silent voice, the humble heart, and the fire of new love. Nirvana, Tao, loyalty to loyalty, and rebirth are permanent standards for the full life of man."[66]

There are hints too that the Cross of Reality is a developmental model. We are plopped into the midst of a history with a past that is not of our choosing, addressed as "thou"; at adolescence we develop the inner self-consciousness of "I," but we move to a future when we form the "we" of marriage. When the story of our lives is complete, we may be examined as an "object," from the outside.[67]

---

65. *CF*, 177-190.

66. *CF*, 190-1.

67. At times, it appears that Rosenstock-Huessy attempts to organize everything in this fourfold grid. The parts of speech correspond to the four points of the Cross, verbs with the past, adjectives with the future, pronouns with the inner and nouns with the outer. Four senses correlate as well: Smell evokes the past, hearing responds to the call of the future, touch is an inner sense, and vision puts us in contact with the external world. Arts stretch out in four directions: drama toward the past, music pulling toward the future, architecture establishing inner spaces, and painting engaging the outer world. Church history develops along these lines in more than one way. The "soul church" of the early church (past) gives way to the "culture church" (future) to the "mind church" (inner) and opening to the "nature church" (outer) (Morgan, *Speech and Society*, 142n12). The church is orga-

As this makes clear, the Cross of Reality is intimately connected with Rosenstock-Huessy's grammatical sociology and his theory of names. A name, he argues, places us at the crossroads of the Cross of Reality. Drawn from the past, it calls us to continuity with our heritage; a name gives us a model to strive to achieve in the future. A name identifies us with the inside of the community, and our name is the mark of our identity as we cross the boundary to the outside of the community. The various moods and types of grammar also correspond to the cross in various ways. The imperative "you" is a voice from the past; the narrative "we" takes us together into the future; the subjective "I" is an expression of the inner man; and outside we deal with various "its." If any of these forms of speech fails, human life is impoverished and human society cannot function. If any of these forms of speech colonizes beyond its proper

---

nized around the poles of liturgy, papacy, theology, and monasticism, each of which overcomes one of the "fortresses of life" in Jerusalem, Rome, Athens, and Egypt (Morgan, *Speech and Society*, 142-3n4). Sexual difference is a difference of orientation in the cross of reality. Men tend to move along the spatial axis, women along the temporal. With no women to link to the past and be fruitful for the future, a purely male community like the monastery of Mount Athos secures a space of timeless immutability. Women are brides in the past, mothers of the future; men are suitors within, possessors without (Morgan, *Speech and Society*, 21-2). Rosenstock-Huessy applies this paradigm to business in *Multiformity of Man*, 4; to family life in various ways in the lectures mentioned in the previous note; to body, mind, soul, and office/role; to different forms of "play" or leisure.

sphere, we again face a personal and social crisis. We cannot deal with our children or spouse as "its."[68]

V. Conclusion

For Rosenstock-Huessy, the specific cross of Jesus reveals the meaning of the general Cross of Reality. There are not two crosses, but ultimately only one. Every human being is stretched out on the Cross of Reality, between the obligations imposed by the past and the desire for the future. Every decent child wants to honor his parents, and yet refuses to relive the life of his parents. Pulled between parental obligations and future hopes, he lives in anguish. Every thoughtful human being dreams of a different world, but finds the world reluctant to comply with his dreams. And thus he is stretched between inner and outer.

This, as I say, is a universal experience. What Jesus reveals is that abundant life is found precisely in being stretched between past and future. Abundant life is not found in an enclave of the conservative past, or in the exuberance of a titillating present, or in a cell of the revolutionary future. Abundant life is not found in retreat to contemplation or in self-forgetting activism.

Abundant life is found when, in faith and hope, we submit to being torn between past and future, inside and outside, and see it as a gateway to renewal. Abundant life

---

68. Morgan, *Speech and Society*, 6.

on the Cross of Reality comes through the cross of Jesus, when, torn by past and future, by inside and outside, we hope against hope for transfiguration.

CHAPTER THREE

GRAMMAR ON THE CROSS

Inspired in part by the obsession with language in modern philosophy, theology has recently been negotiating a "linguistic turn." Fergus Kerr has sketched out the contours of a theology after Wittgenstein,[1] Kevin Vanhoozer's work in hermeneutics and theological method employs speech-act theory,[2] and John R. Betz has published a number of

---

1. *Theology After Wittgenstein*, rev. ed. (London: SPCK, 1997).

2. *Is There a Meaning in this Text?* (Apollos, 1998); *First Theology: God, Scripture, and Hermeneutics* (Downers Grove: InterVarsity, 2002); *The Drama of Doctrine: A Canonical-Linguistic Approach to Christian The-

articles on the great *Sprachdenker*, J. G. Hamann.[3] In a somewhat different vein, James K. A. Smith has formulated a series of theological responses to the challenges posed by postmodern treatments of language.[4] Alongside these developments, biblical scholars have given increasingly sophisticated attention to issues of language and hermeneutics.[5]

In this frenzy of work, one important precursor to the linguistic turn of theology has gone almost entirely unnoticed, namely, the German-American philosopher and sociologist, Eugen Rosenstock-Huessy. Rosenstock-Huessy's grammatical sociology has been the subject of one book-length treatment, but that book is now two decades old

---

ology (Westminster/John Knox, 2005). Michael Horton also employs speech-act theory in his *Covenant and Eschatology: The Divine Drama* (Westminster/John Knox, 2002).

3. "Enlightenment Revisited: Hamann as the First and Best Critic of Kant's Philosophy," *Modern Theology* 20 (2004), 291-301; "Hamann's London Writings: The Hermeneutics of Trinitarian Condescension," *Pro Ecclesia* 14 (2005), 191-234. See also John Milbank, "The Linguistic Turn as a Theological Turn," in *The Word Made Strange: Theology, Language, and Culture* (London: Blackwell, 1997), ch. 4.

4. *The Fall of Interpretation: Philosophical Foundations for a Creational Hermeneutic* (Downers Grove: InterVarsity, 2000); *Speech and Theology: Language and the Logic of Incarnation* (London: Routledge, 2002); *Jacques Derrida: Live Theory* (Continuum, 2005).

5. For example, see Anthony Thiselton, *Two Horizons* (Grand Rapids: Eerdmans, 1980); *New Horizons in Hermeneutics* (Grand Rapids: Zondervan, 1992).

and, helpful as it is, does not begin to exhaust the richness of Rosenstock-Huessy's writings on language and does not highlight some of the most important theological implications of Rosenstock-Huessy's work.[6] An overtly Christian thinker, Rosenstock-Huessy developed his sociology from the categories of grammar and theology, challenging modernity's rationalisms and reductionisms along the way. His work is worthy of fresh attention from a new generation of theologians.

This essay does not pretend to examine every aspect of Rosenstock-Huessy's writings on language, speech, and grammar. Instead, I aim to highlight several central themes of that corpus, and to show how language participates, according to Rosenstock-Huessy, in the Cross that he sees as the central reality of human life.

I

Two main passions drive the whole of Rosenstock-Huessy's work on language. First, he aims to heal the breach that has opened up in Western humanity during the modern period. He describes this breach in various ways, but in one dimension it is a war between science and theology. Rosenstock-Huessy offers grammar as the master science that can unite theology and science in one overall framework. His reasoning is this: Language is the main medium of social

---

6. Morgan, *Speech and Society.*

exchange, and grammar is language come to self-consciousness. Thus, grammar has a right to be considered the master social science. Since both theology and natural sciences are social practices, mediated through language, they are legitimately considered as branches of grammar.[7] This might seem to be a demotion of theology to a subordinate place beneath grammar but what Rosenstock-Huessy is aiming for is a promotion of theology to the full rank of a science. Simultaneously, the grammatical method places limits on natural science, demonstrating that natural science is only the science of spatial reality rather than a science that encompasses reality.[8]

One of the premises of this argument is that science is dependent on articulated speech: "Only when we speak to others (or, for that matter, to ourselves), do we delineate an inner space or circle in which we speak, from the outer world about which we speak. It is by articulated speech that the true concept of space, and that it is being divided into an outer and inner sphere, comes into being."[9] Rosenstock-Huessy is aiming at three things here. First, he insists that speech makes space meaningful because speech articulates and interprets space. Until we speak, we have not

---

7. *Speech and Reality* (Norwich, VT: Argo Books, 1969), 9, 18. Hereafter cited as *SR*.

8. *SR*, 20.

9. *SR*, 21.

clarified what realm natural sciences are going to deal with. Science thus is subordinate to grammar. Specifically, second, articulated speech divides an individual ("I") or corporate "inner space" ("we") from the "outer space" about which we talk ("they" or "it"). Contrary to Cartesian conceptions, space is not mere external extension, but is dual, inner and outer, and this reality is evident in our grammar. Science, third, has its say in the realm of outer space, and this means that "the space of science is *a posteriori*, and just one half of the complete phenomenon of space." The human character of space is not evident in this outer realm, which we confront as an "it." The "truly human phenomenon of space is found in the astounding fact that grammar unites people within one common inner space,"[10] as we form social relations by speaking to one another. In this way, Rosenstock-Huessy seeks to bring natural science into a human sphere, and to show that it has a legitimate, but limited, sphere of operation.

Theology is, by contrast, a temporally oriented science. It is concerned with the historical events of incarnation, cross, and resurrection, and by emphasizing man's response to God's call and command and man's transformation as a result of that call, it is focused on the temporal dimension of human existence. As a temporal science, theology is as dependent upon articulated speech as the spatial natural

---

10. *SR*, 21.

sciences. Like space, time becomes articulated through human speech, through grammar: "It is we who decide what belongs to the past and what shall be part of the future."[11]

In short, through the grammatical method, Rosenstock-Huessy intends to show how his socio-grammatical slogan, *Respondeo etsi mutabor,* encompasses both the medieval theological *credo ut intelligam* and the modern scientific *cogito ergo sum.*[12]

Along similar lines, Rosenstock-Huessy proposes that elevating grammar to the master science challenges the primacy of Greek abstract logic that has dominated Western thinking for centuries. For Rosenstock-Huessy, the primacy of logic is a grammatical phenomenon, the primacy of the indicative. Since the Greeks, the indicative, in the form of "This is an answer," has dominated logic and philosophy, and through them all forms of thought. Other moods of speech are considered derivative, or are forced to conform to the indicative. But the triumph of the indicative, of "This is an answer," is arbitrary. The Bible, Rosenstock-Huessy suggests, discards this Greek logic entirely. Instead of granting primacy to the indicative, the Bible deals in imperatives, interrogatives, optatives, and narratives.[13] Unlike other moods, the indicative detaches

---

11. *SR,* 19

12. *SR,* 24

13. *The Origin of Speech,* 40: "Anybody who reads the first chapter of

the speaker from the listener and from reality. An indicative does not require the presence of the speaker or the hearer in the way that the other forms of speech do:

> My sentence "he is answering him" is much more specific about my own person than the other: "this is an answer." The pure brain is free to say the latter sentence. The whole man—legs, arms, rump and brain—must exist in the same pace and time for the former. The speaker of the sentence "this is an answer" is an abstract being."[14]

Far from being the starting place for logic, the indicative "This is an answer" comes at the end. Syntactically, the indicative is originally used for legal judgments, which are delivered at the end of a trial in which all the other forms of speech have been offered.[15] Further, this secondary form of speech, the indicative, does not operate on the raw material

---

Genesis or the last chapter of Revelation can test our assertion that Greek logic is discarded in favor of a logic in which all the sentences, Give answer, May I have an answer, You have answered me, He answers, hold equal rank." Hereafter, *The Origin of Speech* will be cited as *OS*.

14. *OS*, 42. Rosenstock-Huessy is emphatic about the involvement of the speaker in his speech. One cannot speak at all without changing himself, as well as his listeners, a fact, Rosenstock-Huessy observes, that all propagandists forget (Morgan, *Speech and Society*, 3).

15. *OS*, 43.

of experience, but always assesses facts that have already been articulated in other moods: "Nobody can tell a tale without exposing the listener to all the associations which accompany every single word. . . . All data is historical and therefore told by somebody to somebody else."[16] Semanticists, logicians, and mathematicians, who deal in indicatives, are "gravediggers" of speech; they can only deal with speech after it is already dead. The grammatical method enables Rosenstock-Huessy not only to challenge the colonial ambitions of the natural sciences and modern rationalism, but the modern myth of pure objectivity.

Rosenstock-Huessy's second driving interest is his conviction that speech provides the means for integrating the often conflicting demands of human life, individual and social, which he describes in terms of what he calls the "Cross of Reality."[17] All human beings, Rosenstock-Huessy argues, are stretched out in a cruciform human experience, an experience that always involves the agony of being pulled in various directions at once. The Cross of Reality has a horizontal axis, which represents time, with "past" and "future" at the ends, and a vertical axis, which represents space, with "inside" and "outside" at the two poles. We live our lives in the center of this cross. We have obligations to the past that must be honored, but are equally

---

16. *OS*, 44.

17. For a discussion of some aspects of this paradigm, see chapter 2.

obligated to respond to the call to form a new future. Both demands are legitimate, and living well means dancing gracefully between them. Time as humanly experienced is always the product of the past and future, never a simple "present" moment. Spatially, experience is divided between an inner realm of thought and desire and an outer world, and socially between an "in-group" and an "out-group." Both our desires and the world outside us make their legitimate demands, and if we want to remain sane, we have to find some way to integrate these demands. Both our in-group and out-group lay obligations on us, and we have to find some way to unite these demands, if we are not going to be torn apart by the cross of life.

Rosenstock-Huessy employs this model in many ways, among them as a tool for analyzing the main forms of social crisis. Social evils, he says, can be reduced to four main types—war, revolution, anarchy, and decadence. Each of these is a crisis in regard to one pole or axis of the Cross of Reality. Anarchy is a crisis "inside" the closed circle of the community,[18] while war is a social crisis between the inner group and some strangers. War and anarchy occur along the vertical axis of the cross, along the border line that "like the skin of an individual animal, cuts the world of space into two parts, one inner, one outer."[19] Crises can

---

18. *SR*, 12.

19. *SR*, 13.

also occur along the temporal axis. "Decadence" or "tyranny" is a failure of the older generation, the past, to initiate and inspire the young, the future. Decadence occurs when elders "do not have the stamina of converting the next generation to their own aims and ends." It means "to be unable to reach the future, in body or mind or soul. The decadence of an older generation condemns the younger generation to barbarism. Decadence of parents leaves children without heritage."[20] "Revolution" occurs when "the future generation does violence to the existing order and to the people formed in and by the past. The old are 'liquidated,' 'eliminated,' because they are considered 'past men.'"[21]

Rosenstock-Huessy describes these social evils as failures of speech that can only be healed by renewed speech. Wars occur when speech ceases between one group and another; peace is established when "people who have not been on speaking terms, begin speaking again." Decadence occurs when "the old no longer have the enthusiasm for teaching the young their own faith," and only a renewal of teaching can heal decadence. Anarchy is a "lack of unanimity, of common inspiration." Though the same words are used, "the words (like justice, welfare, commonwealth) do not have an identical meaning among men." When revolutions occur, "all the language and traditions of the past

---

20. *SR*, 12-13.

21. *SR*, 13.

are devaluated like an obsolete currency."[22] In every case all the social evils "hurt language," and they must do so because "language is the weapon against those four social ills." The four evils "dismantle society" by destroying one of the corners of its fortress, but "all speech defends these four fronts."[23]

As this shows, Rosenstock-Huessy has a fairly expansive notion of what "speech" involves. It includes chat, but also all other uses of language, including song, prayer, judicial sentencing, legal declarations, performative utterances, etc. Four "styles of speech" in particular heal the four diseases of language and the four crisis of social order:

> Men reason, men pass laws, men tell stories, men
> sing. The external world is reasoned out, the future
> is ruled, the past is told, the unanimity of the inner

---

22. *SR*, 14.

23. *SR*, 14-15. Rosenstock-Huessy gives a more thorough treatment of this in the opening chapter of *The Origin of Speech*. There he acknowledges that reducing great social crises to "failures of speech" may appear to be a trivialization. But he responds by suggesting that these problems seem bigger than speech precisely because the "plenitude of speech" has dried up (*OS*, 17), and that if speech would be renewed, the social evils would be recognizable for what they are— speech crises. He also makes the argument that the solutions point to the nature of the disease: Wars are remedied by listening, revolutions by re-formulating, economic crises by trust, and decadence by new representatives (*OS*, 17).

circle is expressed in song. People speak together in articulated language because they fear decay, anarchy, war, and revolution. The energies of social life are compressed into words. The circulation of articulated speech is the lifeblood of society. Through speech, society sustains its time and space axes.[24]

Relations with the outside are re-established through reason; the future is secured by legislative speech; men tell stories to preserve the past; and we sing together as a way of renewing mutual inspiration, to breathe the same breath together.

Rosenstock-Huessy's second driving motivation is his sense that human society is torn apart by failures of speech, by failures to embrace the full range of speech and its full power. These failures of speech are not, in modernity, accidental, but arise from some of the fundamental premises of modern thought and the fundamental habits of modern social life. He proposes the grammatical method not only as a means for healing the antinomies of modern thought, but for healing the ills of modern society. He aims to demonstrate the political import of grammar by displaying speech on the Cross of Reality.

---

24. *SR*, 16.

II

Before examining speech on the Cross directly, we need to highlight a few other assumptions and implications of the grammatical method. One of the main assumptions of Rosenstock-Huessy's grammatical method is that modern linguistics, and modern philosophy, go off track from the outset by making the Ego the center of philosophy, linguistics, or psychology. As he explains in his early essay, "The Practical Knowledge of the Soul," this view is embodied already in Greek grammar, which makes the "I" the "first person." As he points out, "all our experience teaches us exactly the opposite of this Greek premise, that the single 'I' is primary." A child develops by "gradually stak[ing] out its borders as an independent entity," by siphoning out the "thousand cares, impressions, and influences which surround, flow around, and beset it." What a child first recognizes is not a world, nor father and mother, but "that it is spoken to": "It is smiled at, entreated, rocked, comforted, punished, given presents, or nourished. It is first a 'you' to a powerful being outside itself—above all to its parents."[25] Goethe said a father is always his daughter's first god; Rosenstock-Huessy agrees, adding that "He is so because he is present for his daughter before her own 'I' is, and because he bestows on her the consciousness of herself, by address-

---

25. "Practical Knowledge of the Soul" (Norwich, VT: Argo Books, 1988), 16. Cited hereafter as *PKS*.

ing her as 'you.'"[26] Before we can articulate anything about our own existence, we hear "others say that we exist and mean something to them." Thus, "we develop self-consciousness by receiving commands and being judged from outside. In the face of these commands and judgments, we perceive that we are someone special, and being something different or special is the fundamental experience of the 'I.'"[27] We become Egos in response to commands. Hence, the original mood of our social speech is not the indicative but the imperative. And the first person of social speech is not the grammatical first person, but the second person of personal address. A child may describe himself in third person, but in response to a command, he is forced to a "Yes" or "No." In these answers, the child realizes himself as an individual: "These two words are only apparently mere interjections. Actually, they are expressions of the truly divine 'I' personality, the foundations of the omnipotence given us. To say 'yes' and 'no' means to create and resist, to suffer and to create suffering."[28]

In sum,

All self-recognition, all of an "I-s" self-knowledge, is produced by summons, by an individual's defi-

---

26. *PKS*, 16.

27. *PKS*, 16.

28. *PKS*, 17.

nite feeling that a concrete challenge has hit home. His childhood gods want, as do those of his father and mother, or of anyone else. . . . The imperative may erupt from unexpected sources, but it is always the imperative which forces a soul to come forward and which unfolds its powers into the realm of the body as well as that of the spirit.[29]

Rosenstock-Huessy makes large claims for grammar and his grammatical method, and one might be tempted to think that he is using "grammar" in an extended metaphorical sense, as George Lindbeck does when he speaks of doctrine as a kind of "grammar."[30] But Rosenstock-Huessy literally means *grammar* when he writes about grammar as the master science. As noted above, he wants to tease out what our grammar says about language, since language is the binding power of social relations, and grammar is language come to self-consciousness. He complains in various places about the way grammar is taught to schoolchildren, and suggests ways in which our teaching of grammar distorts and veils the social reality and power of speech. He complains particularly about the "Alexandrian table of grammar" that every beginning Latin student employs:

---

29. *PKS*, 17.

30. *The Nature of Doctrine: Religion and Theology in a Postliberal Age* (Westminster/John Knox, 1984).

amo, amas, amat, etc. The problem with this is that "all persons are put through the same drill. They all seem to speak in the same manner." But the notion that "all these sentences can and should be treated as of the same social character" is a "fatal error."[31] It is not true that we can string out first, second, and third persons in a line, as if each were socially and personally equivalent: "In our modern society, *amo* and *amas* are treated as though they too were mere statements of fact as *amat*."[32]

In reality, the social consequences of *amo* and *amas* are radically different from the social consequences of *amat*.[33] We may utter "*amat*" or "*amatur*" without any stake in the sentence we utter. In fact, these can be uttered only by someone on the outside of the relationship of love, only by someone for whom the love spoken of is, or has become, powerless. Third-person discussion of love, Rosenstock-Huessy says, is "no small achievement" as it "neutralizes the power of love." If we speak of God in the third person, we attempt something similar with Him: "God in prayer, God in the ten commandments—is the living God. God as the object of theology is powerless, a mere third person."[34] Rosenstock-Huessy emphasizes that the nega-

---

31. *SR*, 100.

32. *SR*, 108.

33. *SR*, 100.

34. *SR*, 101.

tion involved in the use of the third person is a double negation. It not only abstracts the speaker from his speech, but abstracts the listener as well. An objective statement "is a two-fold negation of relationship."[35] In a third-person utterance, neither the speaker nor listener is involved in the truth or falsity of the statement. Bill and Ted might debate the truth of *amat* concerning Al, but the outcome of the debate is indifferent to Bill and Ted. Only when we recognize this double negation can we see "the abyss between the objective third person in *amat* and the two conversing people who exchange their views about him as subject and preject."[36]

Amo, on the contrary, is risky business because it involves both speaker and hearer. Whenever we say *amo*, we admit that we are involved in the action or passion of which we speak. We cannot say "*amo*" without a self-commitment, in an off-hand, detached way. Saying "*amo*" is a confession, and anyone who speaks that way "runs a risk which he does not run in speaking of somebody else! He runs the risk of destroying the act to which the sentence testifies."[37] A man who says *amo* risks interference—from a rival, from parents, from the law, sometimes, as with Lysander and Hermia in *A Midsummer Night's Dream*, from

---

35. *SR*, 101.

36. *SR*, 102.

37. *SR*, 102.

all three at once. A man who acts as he speaks runs the risk of being stopped in his act.[38] Not only is *amo* riskier and radically more self-involving than *amat*, but it is also an act on the social world in a way that *amat* is not. A report that says "*amat*" does not change anything, but simply describes what is already the case. The third-person is conservative. But "the speaker of a sentence in the first person cannot help changing his own social situation simply by divulging any act, thought, feeling, intention of himself."[39] Because of the risks, *amo* tends to be uttered in the safety of a private space, where the lover is protected from immediate interference.[40]

To utter the first person, one must break through a natural reluctance to express what is within. To utter a second person sentence, we have to break through the hearer's reluctance to hear. To speak a sentence in the second person is always to assume an office; there is inevitably an implicit hierarchy in saying "you." Even if the "you" is as simple as "You have bad breath," it assumes that the speaker has some authority to speak, or it will be greeted with a response ranging between indifference and a punch in the snoot: "Why is advice unasked for never given successfully? Because it has no power to unlock

---

38. *SR*, 103.

39. *SR*, 103.

40. *SR*, 104.

the recipient's ear."[41] To utter a second-person sentence, we have to convert the hearer into a listener."[42] In sum,

> the speaker of *amo* has made up his mind to break his silence about himself although this means running the risk of intervention. The listener of *amas* has made up his mind to invite interference. The speaker and listener of *amat* have nothing to readjust in their own political attitude before they listen to this fact. They are neither defying nor inviting interference in their own affairs.[43]

All three types of statements are debatable, but in different registers: "whereas *amat* is debatable as to truth, *amas* is debatable as to authority, *amo* is debatable as to wisdom."[44] We cannot use the same standards to evaluate the three types of utterances; "truth-value" is the right standard for the third-person, but not for the first or second.[45] Against the centuries-long reduction of dialectic to third-person indicatives, Rosenstock-Huessy sketches a dialectic that is multiform, three-dimensional.

---

41. *SR*, 106.

42. *SR*, 106.

43. *SR*, 106.

44. *SR*, 107.

45. *SR*, 107.

The social sciences are off-kilter, Rosenstock-Huessy argues, because of "the false dogmas planted in the grammar school and high school," because the social and political contours of real language are flattened out into a grammatical table. As soon as students become self-conscious about language, they are trained in wrong views of human society, and Rosenstock-Huessy argues that "it is simpler to tell the truth from the beginning" by discarding the Alexandrian table of grammar. When we reduce all persons to the third person, we destroy human society: "Human relations thrive where we attribute secrets of communication and loyalties of listening. Human relations die when all our statements only contribute facts."[46] The Alexandrian list teaches children "to believe that I love and you love and we love may be said in a similarly flat voice as he loves or they love." The result is predictable: "our educated classes have come to deny emphasis."[47]

---

46. *SR*, 109.

47. *SR*, 111. Rosenstock-Huessy reinforces this point by introducing a fourth focus of discussion, the plural "we." By uttering "we," we establish unity between speaker and listener, and this is the driving force of history: "All history is the tale of acts in which some speaker and some listener become one." History is only history if it is "the inside story of a We group" (*SR*, 109). In part, Rosenstock-Huessy is arguing that human beings can have a sense of a unified history only through telling history as a series of "we" events. When history is told in the third person, it proliferates: "'They' can be said of any group and nation, big or small. Harlem has a history, the Bronx has

One of the key distinctions in Rosenstock-Huessy's grammatical sociology is that between names and words. In his brief discussion of this distinction in *The Christian Future*, he begins with an expression of his horror at John Dewey's notion that "We have to find another set of words to formulate the moral ideal."[48] What motivates action, Rosenstock-Huessy protests, is not a "set of words" but a name, a sacred name. Liberalism is paralyzed because it mocks the sacredness of names, but at the same time wants to motivate us to act, and act strenuously, for something. But the only thing that will motivate is a call that confronts us in the "name" of some hope for the future.[49] Dewey and all idealists think that names always function like they do in commerce, but there is an enormous difference between a "Lincoln" car and the "Lincoln" who lends his name to the car. Lincoln became a usable commercial word because in his life Lincoln combined words and deeds:

---

a history, Manhattan has a history, it would appear. The subdivisions of a third-person-history crave multiplication" into a multicultural extravaganza (*SR*, 110). Earlier historians didn't write third-person history; Thucydides, Tacitus, Gregory of Tours, and Voltaire each "felt himself a faithful child of history which he tried to rewrite as 'our history'" (*SR*, 110).

48. *CF*, 7.

49. *CF*, 8.

Names are so sacred because they constitute the unity of the conflict of words and deeds in human life. Names are priceless; words have their price. Words can be definite, names must have an infinite appeal. Names must make us act in ways which seemed unbelievable before they were done; words express the things which are to be had at a known price in figures.[50]

Elsewhere, Rosenstock-Huessy argues that names are not labels but rather "promises and commands, invitations to the bearer and to the spirit invoked upon the bearer and to the community calling the bearer by this spirit's power."[51] Names are taboos, protecting a "child against abuse by its parents" as "an amulet and a charm." They are appeals to responsibility. And they are means for offering praise to God.[52] A name, like all genuine speech, is always a triune event, involving the public, the speaker, and the inspiration that animates the speaker. To name involves affirming the truth of what is said, being willing to stand up for what is said, and insisting that what is said should be accepted by everyone in the community.[53] To name is to face the pub-

---

50. *CF*, 8.

51. *OS*, 34.

52. *OS*, 35.

53. *OS*, 34-35.

lic, to call the one named, and to invoke a spirit that will enable the one bearing the name to fulfill the calling.

Proper names, Rosenstock-Huessy suggests, have an imperatival quality, and therefore names form us just as imperatives do: "A person's being addressed by his own distinguishing proper name precedes any thinking about himself the 'I' may do." To say "I" is to become an object to oneself, but that doesn't occur until we have first been addressed. A "man who is distinguished by a proper name, unlike the classifiable things of the outside world: trees, tables, stones, or houses," is able to come to consciousness of himself, to resist and say, "Yes" or "No." The "I" is a product of this resistance, but it presumes that the man has been addressed by name.[54]

III

Against this background, Rosenstock-Huessy assembles his grammatical material on the four poles of the Cross of Reality discussed above. He begins a phenomenological discussion of the "four responsibilities in speaking" by describing his encounter with a boy across the fence at his home. He called out "OOOOh," and the boy answered with a "prolonged oooooooooooh." This exchange was an exchange of sound, but it does not qualify as speech. Why not? Rosenstock-Huessy says that it lacked two essential characteristics

---

54. *PKS*, 17.

of speech—names and answers. For speech to take place, we must have a name of the person addressed, and we must have an answer that is not merely a repetition of what was said in the initial address.[55] Analyzing this simple example yields two basic principles. First, if speech takes place only by using names and proper terms, then speech is always a participation in an ages-long stream of communication: "We never start all over again when we speak. Because the success of the speech depends on its being 'proper.' Proper language yields more power to his owner than property."[56] Speech always flows from the past, which is one end of the Cross of Reality.

The second lesson is that speech is never repetition between two speakers, but always involves both "identity and variation."[57] A response, to be a response of speech, must be consistent with the speaker's intentions: It does no good to argue with someone who has merely expressed his internal desires, or to agree factually with an imperative. The speaker sets the terms of the exchange by the mode in which he gives his initial speech.[58] Yet, though the responder must respond in kind, his response can never be mere repetition of the initial speech, else "they are a chorus

---

55. *SR*, 47-48.

56. *SR*, 48.

57. *SR*, 49.

58. *SR*, 49.

and not interlocutors."[59] Hence, "Language means the liberty between two people to modulate in complementary ways one and the same word or idea or topic or language." Whether strangers are talking about the weather, scholars are debating a point, an attorney is arguing a case in court, the two sides are always "committed to a ballet which they execute together": "No party speech, no theoretical innovation, no scientific discovery, no part of any dialogue in the world make sense if it is not understood as a variation of something the speaker and public have and hold in common, yet as a variation by which the speaker leads into a new future."[60] Speech, all speech, also stretches out to the future pole of the Cross.

Already, we are most of the way to seeing grammar on Cross of Reality. From the two features of his exchange with the neighbor boy, Rosenstock-Huessy draws the conclusion that his speech also expressed a desire ("I wished to attract the boy's attention"), and that his call was an "external process." When I speak, my body causes vibrations on the air, which reach a listener's ear. When these two observations are combined with the analysis of the encounter above, we have four dimensions of speech. Speech is always at all four poles of the Cross of Reality: It uses proper words (past), expects an answer that varies coherently with the

---

59. *SR*, 50.

60. *SR*, 50.

address (future), expresses a desire (inside), and is an external process (outside). We look to the four winds whenever we open our mouths: Back to earlier uses, forward to an answer; we express a desire from within, and initiate an external process, changing the world outside. Every time we speak, "we assert our being alive because we occupy a center from which the eye looks backward, forward, inward, and outward."[61]

This grammatical cross works at several levels, organizing the sociology of grammatical persons, moods, and principal parts. Though there are variations on this model in various works, Rosenstock-Huessy's basic themes can be summarized as follows:

	Past	Inside	Outside	Future
Parts	adjective[62]	pronoun	noun	verb[63]
Moods	narrative	optative/ subjunctive	indicative	imperative
Person	1st plural	1st singular	third	second

---

61. *SR*, 52.

62. Adjectives, Rosenstock-Huessy claims, describe unfamiliar new things in familiar terms. What is that, we ask wonderingly? And we can arrive at an answer by noting that it is big, red, hairy, sharp-toothed.

63. Verbs speak of an unfinished world, of a world in process, and thus point to the future.

As he makes explicit in *The Origin of Speech*, moods gravitate toward one or the other persons, and these mood-persons gravitate toward a particular mode of language and a particular experience of time:[64]

Dramatic	lyrical	epical	logical
(imperative)	(subjunctive)	(narrative)	(classifying)
2d	1st	3d plural/	infinitive

These various moods and persons, in turn, are also linked to various disciplines and courses of study. The grammatical method thus comes into its own as the master science:

Narrative	Imperative	Lyric	Judgment
Tradition/truth	ethics, goodness	aesthetics	science
Loyalty	movements	beauty	system
History	politics	poetry	objectivism
Literature	revolution	subjectivism	mathematics
Evolution			skepticism
Liturgy	Law	Art	science

---

64. *OS*, 69.

These charts not only demonstrate Rosenstock-Huessy's vision of grammar as a master science, but also begin to show how he sees speech as the existential means for integrating the conflicting but legitimate demands of the Cross of Reality. Torn by the Cross, we must speak or else we die. Speech is a response to the crisis of living at the center of the Cross. It is our human cry of dereliction, but in that cry we become whole. As he says,

> we speak lest we break down under the strain of this quadrilateral. We speak in an attempt to ease this strain. To speak, means to unify, to simplify, to integrate life. Without this effort, we would go to pieces in either too much inner, unuttered desire, or too many impressions made upon us by our environment, too many petrified formulas fettering us from the past, or too much restless curiosity for the future.[65]

Poetic this may be, but what does it mean? Rosenstock-Huessy argues that his grammatical method reveals speech as the integrating act of human existence. Through the grammatical method, human beings become self-conscious of our place "in history (backward), world (outward),

---

65. *SR*, 18.

society (inward), and destiny (forward)",[66] and becoming self-conscious we are capable of living as integrated beings even while torn on the Cross. Speech itself gives us this direction and orientation, but grammar, which is language come to self-consciousness, provides "an additional consciousness of this power of direction and orientation" available in speech.[67] Speaking integrates inside and outside by articulating the boundary between them, and by extending and contracting the boundaries. As we speak, the "outside" world becomes ever more thinkable, incorporated into our inner world. Speech integrates past and future, as the command "come" yields to the past tense "he has come."[68]

Language as a whole manifests its integrating and unifying power, since the same language can be used to express desire, to analyze a scientific experiment, to report a past event, or to command a future series of actions.[69] Equally, every act of speech integrates all four poles of the Cross of Reality. When we speak, we implicitly appeal to the past, seek to shape the future, put an inner desire out into the open, make a statement about the external world. Each act of speech makes us a leader (imperative, future), an observer (indicative, outside), a historian (narrative, past), and a

---

66. *SR*, 18.

67. *SR*, 18.

68. *SR*, 55.

69. *SR*, 64.

poet (optative, inside). Speech thus enables us to "recognize all events in time and space as coherent."[70] Language always contains "scientific, political, historical (or institutional), and poetic elements." Human beings specialize in one or the other mode of speech, but even in our specialized area (science, politics, history, poetry) we speak in all four modes or we fail to be human. To speak is always an act of faith that the demands of the Cross can be integrated, since all language assumes the "unity of all these four types of language."[71]

In a brilliant essay analyzing the implications of Augustine's *de Magistro*, Rosenstock-Huessy uses teaching as a paradigm to demonstrate how speech articulates and integrates time. Teaching requires a coordination of time, the schedules of students and teachers. For teaching to happen, they have to show up in the classroom at the same time. But they do not show up as "contemporaries" but as "distemporaries." The teacher is always "older," if not in actual age at least in his exposure to the material; the student is always "younger" because he has never been exposed to the material or because he has not been exposed to it so deeply as the teacher. "Old" and "young" are not biological but social facts. The reality of teaching is a sign that time can be synchronized, and old/past and young/future can be har-

---

70. *SR*, 55.

71. *SR*, 56.

monized in a third type of time, the time of the classroom. Distemporaries can live together only "if they admit that they form a succession, if they affirm their quality of belonging to different times." This mutual recognition is what forms the present. The present, whether in the classroom or anywhere else, is not natural; naturally, the "present" is the razor's edge between past and future, the wisp that vanishes before we have uttered the word. This natural present is not the present of human experience. The human present is a social fact, a social construct, the fruit of the verbal efforts of the old and young, past and future, to coordinate their distemporaneity.[72]

Speech also integrates life along the spatial axis. By speaking, we dissolve the boundaries, the "skins" that separate insides from outsides. When I express my individual wishes, the boundary between my heart and my listener dissolves, and we form a union despite our spatial division. When a Tutsi speaks to a Hutu in a way that a Hutu can understand, the boundaries between tribe and tribe also dissolve. Speech creates the possibility for the union of individuals into a society, and for the union of societies into a single humanity.

None of these modes of language can flourish without the others, and when one or another gains primacy, social

---

72. "Man Must Teach," in *Rosenstock-Huessy Papers, Volume I* (Norwich, VT: Argo Books, 1981).

and personal evils are inevitable. Scientists and philosophers have expended a good bit of effort in an attempt to reduce all speech to scientific and philosophical terms. Normal language is "imperfect" in their view, because it's full of statements that cannot easily be forced into the mold of indicative factual assertions. So, philosophers and scientists abandon normal speech in favor of mathematics or symbolic logic.[73] This "secondary language" of critical reflection is useful because it offers the possibility of "re-thinking of the things said before." But when one is a professional "second-thinker," he's liable to "superimpose this, his own aim, upon everybody who handles language and condemn all first and primary language as being a misfit." Thus, scientific and logical language filters out into everyday speech, and language as a whole becomes more analytical.[74] This is socially dangerous, as is any effort to impose one pole of the Cross of Reality on all speech: "A merely scientific, or a purely educational society or a ritualistic society or a poetical society—everyone of them would cease to live."[75]

Modernity inhibits this integration because it reduces all speech to scientific, external, indicative speech. But science and philosophy cannot even operate by their own premises, since scientific and philosophical speech are nev-

---

73. *SR*, 58.

74. *SR*, 59.

75. *SR*, 61.

er simply "externally" oriented anyway. We do not live by "reflection or by formula, alone," but instead find that our language is full of "suggestive invitation," the imperative "Come" that Rosenstock-Huessy places under the heading of "politics" and "education," speech oriented to the future. However analytical they aim to be, "the pure scientist cannot help using suggestive invitations." Scientists are politicians too, since

> there is no science without the political and educational act. For the scientific thought is trying to make its way into the world, and that means changing the world, changing society by getting a hearing, being given a chance, getting an endowment, getting students, becoming a textbook, and taking possession of the brains of unsophisticated young people. The "actus purus" of science makes no sense without the "actus impurus" of publication.[76]

Politics (future), in turn, is inherently poetic (inside). Politics and education, oriented to the future, must be refreshed by the influx of inner speech and desire from writers and prophets, scientists and politicians. A political

---

76. *SR*, 61.

program originates as a poetical dream: "Politics without poetics are a failure."[77]

If one or the other of the poles of the Cross of Reality is ignored, if language operates at only one pole, human life can only wither on the vine:

> The life of mankind does depend on the integrity of all its members to shift between the four ways of speech freely. The liberty of man is to be found in his right to sing, to think, to invite or lead and to celebrate or remember. These four acts cover the four aspects of reality. By these four acts, the artist, the philosopher, the leader and the priest, within every human being, is regenerated daily. Whenever we use articulated speech we are artists, philosophers, leaders and priests of the universe.[78]

IV

Though rarely overt, it seems clear that Rosenstock-Huessy's analysis of the Cross of Grammar, and the integrating power of speech, is at bottom a Christological analysis. Certainly, Rosenstock-Huessy sees Jesus as the integrating Person of time, of all times. Every generation, granted, has to live for itself, "in the spirit of their time," but without some-

77. *SR*, 61.

78. *SR*, 62.

thing to bring unity to the ages, "there still would be the arrogance and the disloyalty and the indifference of the last generation towards all the previous." Jesus put an end to the ancient practice of "ceaseless splitting into new beginnings": "After all these 'afters,' all these juvenile 'waves of the future,' the mere beginner would still have to be converted into the son and heir of all times." Through this kind of "conversion," the seed of a "convergence of all generations" was planted. Jesus "embedded all times, including his own, in one supertime, one eternal present."[79] All men are on the cross, torn in pieces, but "together we may look for a supertime, for the fellowship in which we can relieve each other's crucial split by solidarity." Through fellowship among generations, man "can come home." Supertimes are created by "the faith of every generation," and this faith is "the simple application of the principle of unlocking the doors between the times as practiced by Jesus first."[80]

The whole idea of the "Christian era," Rosenstock-Huessy claims, is the declaration that "Now is the time" and that "today these prophecies are fulfilled in your hearing":

> Jesus became the center of history by *being* the human soul made visible, the Messiah whom the Jews

---

79. *CF*, 189.

80. *CF*, 189.

expected only at the end of history. In this way he introduced the end of time as a directing force in the present. Whereas the Jews identified end and beginning in God and virtually ignored everything in between, Jesus created a historical process in which every year, every day, every present is equally immediate to God because it is equally a meeting point for all the imperfect past and perfecting future. In Jesus the beginnings of antiquity all come to an end and all the ends of modern man make their beginning; the promises of old, to all the nations, are not turned progressively into realizations.[81]

His death and resurrection made Jesus "Founder of the Messianic kingdom." Only by death could He transcend the "old Law" and the responsibilities of a mere child of Abraham. He had only His death "to invest in the future, and his great discovery was that the true future is opened up by the power that survives death. In revealing this power he created man's perfect plasticity on the forward front, his ability to begin anew each day like a new-born child. He redeemed mere birth by revealing it as the fruit of death."[82]

Jesus is the Word who hangs on the Cross of Reality, pulling the four poles, and particularly past and future,

---

81. *CF*, 190.

82. *CF*, 190.

into one united reality, one common present. In His cry of dereliction, the eternal Word shouts the agony of all men, but in that cry of dereliction He also unites all things in and to Himself. Jesus unites me to my world, and unites my group to every other tribe and tongue and nation and people. Jesus the Word is the one in whom, as Paul says, "all things cohere" (Colossians 1:17). In Him are summed up all past ages, and through Him comes an everlasting future. Through the Word made flesh, through divine speech, the Cross of Reality is integrated in one Man. Inspired by that divine speech and the breath of His mouth, filled with the filial speech of the last days, we speak so as to integrate our own lives, lives always still lived out on the cross.

CHAPTER FOUR

THE SOCIAL ARTICULATION OF TIME IN EUGEN ROSENSTOCK-HUESSY

The German-American social philosopher Eugen Rosenstock-Huessy was a *Zeitdenker* as much as a *Sprachdenker*. Indeed, he was the one because he was the other. In his correspondence with Rosenzweig, he wrote that "this temporal character of my thinking is, in fact, the Alpha and Omega from which I grasp everything afresh," and immediately added "Speech reflects this mode of procedure."[1] He agreed with Georg Muller's assessment that his thinking circulat-

---

1. Quoted in Harold Stahmer, *"Speak that I May See Thee!" The Religious Significance of Language* (New York: Macmillan, 1968), 106.

ed around the "trinity" of speech, time, and history: "the speech of individuals and nations, the times of lovers and haters, the history of empires, the church and society as the reflections of the divine trinity."[2]

This focus on temporality was central to his critique of philosophy. Philosophy does not simply take things as they come but has to assemble things together "in one place" as it were, before it begins its work of division, categorization, and analysis. Because of this, philosophy can never be more than a "second impression, an afterthought."[3] After Descartes especially, philosophy deleted temporality, polarizing experience in a spatial subject-object dualism. Even Martin Buber, with whom Rosenstock-Huessy is often associated, failed to give sufficient attention to time. Rosenstock-Huessy agreed with Rosenzweig's complaint that Buber's I-Thou, I-It distinction is "not bound to time and nourished by time."[4] In the Cross of Reality, Rosenstock-Huessy's basic theoretical construct, he redressed these problems by adding a temporal axis to the spatial axis of post-Enlightenment philosophical and scientific thought.

---

2. *Religious Significance*, 9.

3. Quoted in Wayne Cristaudo, "Eugen Rosenstock-Huessy," in *Stanford Encyclopedia of Philosophy*, www.seop.leeds.uk/entries/rosenstock-huessy (2008); cf. also Stahmer, 137.

4. Quoted in Stahmer, 64.

I want to introduce Rosenstock-Huessy the *Zeit-denker* into two contemporary conversations. The first of these concerns the role of time in social theory, the second conversation is recent theological discussion of time. Rosenstock-Huessy has important contributions to make to each conversation. More importantly, though, Rosenstock-Huessy transcends these conversations because he speaks both theology and sociology. Theologians who discuss time rarely think about clocks and calendars; social theorists, on the other hand, have little time for God.[5] Rosenstock-Huessy had time for God and calendars, and offers unique resources for integrating the two discourses.[6]

This chapter proceeds in three stages. First, I briefly summarize recent explorations of time in social theo-

---

5. I assume without argument here that an integrated conception of time needs to include consideration of theological and metaphysical concerns. One direction for defending this conclusion would be to show that a purely immanent social view of time cannot account for the reality of common time, the daily experience that we share time with others. If time is wholly relative to the experiencer or observer, then it is difficult to see how our times could be made to overlap, yet they do. There has to be a unifying point "above" temporal relativity to account for this. This is hardly airtight or complete, but it indicates a direction of argument.

6. Given the limits of my time and my expertise, this chapter is necessarily a selective summary of themes in Rosenstock-Huessy's immense and immensely rich corpus. It would, for instance, be of interest to examine Rosenstock-Huessy's differences with philosophers of temporal experience like Husserl, Heidegger and Sartre.

ry and theology. Then, I examine some themes in Rosen-stock-Huessy's treatment of time. Finally, I return to the twin debates in social theory and theology, this time show-ing Rosenstock-Huessy's peculiar contribution to those debates. I argue that two of his themes are of particular relevance. He challenges the dualistic understanding of time prevalent in the social sciences with his notion of the "multiformity of the present," and he challenges the more implicit dualism of theological accounts of time with his particular interpretation of the biblical phrase "the fullness of time."

I

British sociologist Anthony Giddens charges that "most forms of social theory have failed to take seriously enough not only the temporality of social conduct but also its spatial attributes," so that "neither time nor space have been incor-porated into the centre of social theory." At best, time is part of the "environment" within which social action takes place but is not treated as a component of social action itself.[7]

---

7. Anthony Giddens, *Central Problems in Social Theory: Action, Structure, and Contradiction in Social Analysis* (Berkeley: University of California Press, 1979), 202.

Barbara Adam[8] and Norbert Elias[9] also lament the inattention to time among social scientists, and both claim that social theory has been structured by an implicit dichotomy of social and natural time. With roots in Cartesian philosophy and early modern science, this dualism is reinforced by the disciplinary divisions of the university. According to this paradigm, natural scientists investigate the world as a predictable object and formulate theories concerning the objective reality of time, while social scientists are co-involved in the unpredictable reality they study and construct theories that deal with the subjective meanings that humans project on time.[10] The working definition of time unthinkingly adopted by much social science is either the quasi-timeless absolute time of Newtonian physics or the more accessible regularity of "clock time."[11] On these

---

8. Barbara Adam, "Social Versus Natural Time: A Traditional Distinction Re-Examined," in Michael Young and Thomas Schuller, eds., *The Rhythms of Society* (London: Routledge, 1988); more fully, Adam, *Time and Social Theory* (Philadelphia: Temple University Press, 1990) and Adam, *Time* (Cambridge: Polity Press, 2004).

9. Norbert Elias, *An Essay on Time* (Collected Works of Norbert Elias, vol. 9; Dublin: University College Dublin Press, 1992).

10. For all his attention to the importance of time in social action and structure, Giddens falls into a variation of this dichotomy, arguing that natural scientists stand in a "subject-object" relation to their material and social scientists in a "subject-subject" relation. See the critique of Adam, *Time and Social Theory*, 151.

11. On the other hand, Adam notes a consensus among social theo-

assumptions, objective, and, implicitly, "real" time is "uniform, homogenous," "purely quantitative, shorn of qualitative variations," and is infinitely divisible into smaller units. Social and subjective time, by contrast, consists of irreducible wholes whose rich variety and human meaning depend on the "contents" of time.[12]

There are multiple errors in this construction. To start with the obvious, clock time is not the time of nature. Sunrise and sunset are regular, but their regularities are variable, and all other "natural" clocks are just as variable. Natural time as described by contemporary physics and chronobiology is far more complex and interesting than the time of classical physics. A clock is, of course, a mechanical device, the product of centuries of human ingenuity and artifice. Its dominance in our notions of time is historically recent and was, at the time of its emergence, contested.[13]

---

rists, going back to Durkheim, that "all time is social time." That is, the before and after that is observable in nature is not the same as the reality of past, present, and future time, which exist only for human beings endowed with memory and anticipation. The only time is time symbolically expressed in human society. Adam appeals to recent scientific research that suggests that past, present, and future are integral to physical and biological systems and not merely human.

12. The quotations are taken from Sorokin and Merton, "Social Time: A Methodological and Functional Analysis," quoted in Adam, "Social Versus Natural Time," 202.

13. See Michael O'Malley, *Keeping Watch: A History of American Time* (New York: Penguin, 1990); Lewis Mumford, *The Human Prospect*

"Measuring time" by a clock, as Elias points out,[14] reflects a cultural decision to measure a comparatively irregular continuum (a basketball game, a film, a political speech, a day) by reference to a comparatively regular continuum (the mechanical clock). Industrializing societies that coordinate and synchronize their activities by clock-time have been seduced into regarding clock-time as time *simpliciter*. Elias suggests that social theory can exorcise the bewitching reification of clock time by substituting the verbal form "timing" for the nominalization "time." The burden of much of Adam's work is to break down the dichotomy of natural/social time by introducing social scientists to the insights of relativity theory, dissipative systems, quantum mechanics, and the rhythmics studied by contemporary biologists.

Once the natural/social dichotomy is in place, it is hard to resist the notion that "social time" is somehow less real than "natural time." Social theory operates with the assumption that what we do with and in our times makes no difference to objective, real time itself, which merrily ticks away, indifferent to our attempts to fill it. Several recent theologians have raised similar objections to the modern mechanization, flattening, and "spatialization" of

---

(Boston: Beacon Press, 1955), 3-9; Stephen Kern, *The Culture of Time and Space* (1983, repr., Cambridge: Harvard University Press, 2003).

14. Elias, 69.

time,[15] and other theologians have noted modernity's, and the Christian tradition's, quasi-Gnostic unease with time.[16] Yet, when theologians ask, "How does God relate to time?" they frequently mean the time of physics rather than social time. In *Theology, Music, and Time*, for example, Jeremy Begbie develops a rich theology of time using the resources of music theory, which provides a way of articulating the thickness of real time. No moment is a pure present, but is always emerging from the past and leaning toward the future, as one chord leaves us tipping toward the next, ultimately toward a final resolution. Every moment of time is the intersection of multiple layers of temporal and historical rhythm, just as any moment in a musical composition is simultaneously fits into the sequence of individual notes and chords, the regular recurrence of measures, a metrical sequence, a rhythmic pattern that is not identical to the meter, melodic developments and repetitions, themes with their developments and inversions, and movements. While

---

15. Cathering Pickstock, *After Writing: On the Liturgical Consummation of Philosophy* (Oxford: Blackwell, 1998).

16. Jeremy Begbie, *Theology, Music and Time* (Cambridge: Cambridge University Press, 2000); Colin Gunton, *The One, the Three and the Many: God, Creation, and the Culture of Modernity* (Cambridge: Cambridge University Press, 1993); Douglas Knight, "Jenson on Time," in Colin Gunton, ed., *Trinity, Time, and Church: A Response to the Theology of Robert Jenson* (Grand Rapids: Eerdmans, 2000), 71-79; Knight, *The Eschatological Economy: Time and the Hospitality of God* (Grand Rapids: Eerdmans, 2006).

Begbie's study leaves ample room for the development of an understanding of the multiformity of time, he unfortunately leaves the social aspects of time comparatively undeveloped.[17] Robert Jenson too is fairly obsessed with the God-and-time question. The great difference between Christianity and the religions and refined philosophies of antiquity, he argues, is that for Christianity time and history form the location for the identification of God. Nonetheless, Christian theology has too often been seduced by Hellenistic enticements to escape from time, and to ensure that nothing that "smacks of time" is attributed to God Himself. On the contrary, Jenson argues, God is smacking full of time, and he explores this point most fully when discussing the implications of Trinitarian theology. In the end, however, Jenson too fails to integrate social time-marking into his theology of time (see below, section IV).

Even at their best, most theologians ignore the daily human experience of time, and as a result theologies of time reinforce a central feature of the modern caricature of time that they intend to challenge. They challenge modern flattening of time, but assume that *real* time is indeed homogenous and uniform. The failure to challenge modern

---

17. Begbie, *Theology*, 72, 143. Colin Gunton's discussion of time has a similar gap. Though Gunton claims to be developing an understanding of time that highlights existential and particular dimensions, he writes at a fairly high level of abstraction and mentions clocks and calendars only in a brief paragraph (*The One*, 74-100).

conceptions of time arises from the fact that many offer a theology of time, but not a *social* theology of time.[18] For

---

18. This chapter gives attention to a few very recent theologians who have contributed to the theology of temporality, but the limitation I find in Begbie and Gunton is evident in many others as well. Jurgen Moltmann's *The Coming of God: Christian Eschatology*, trans. Margaret Kohl (Minneapolis: Augsburg/Fortress, 2004) refers to calendrical time only a few times, mostly disparagingly. Barth's thrilling and profound meditations on God's eternity as "time for us" and His insistence on the event-character of God's action have little room for a positive assessment of what he calls "the highly questionable time of our calendar and clocks" (*Church Dogmatics*, I/2 [Edinburgh: T&T Clark, 2004], 59). As a result, theologically significant time is the time of redemptive acts, the time slipping from future to past through the ungraspable present, the time allotted to man. The complexly shaped time between the allotted time of an entire life and the elusive present is missing, though of course most human experience of time takes place precisely in that "between." In short, though Barth highlights the theological depth of time, he leaves the connection of this saturated time with clock time unclear and also leaves the impression that clock-time is precisely what moderns think it is, flat, empty, homogenous. Barth's most extended discussion of time is in *Church Dogmatics* III/2, chapter 47. For a concise summary of Barth's theology of time, see Eberhard Busch, *The Great Passion: An Introduction to Karl Barth's Theology*, trans. Geoffrey Bromiley (Grand Rapids: Eerdmans, 2004), ch. 10. Von Balthasar brings out a social dimension of time ("our time"), but links it closely to death and ignores the most quotidian social organization of time (*Theo-Drama: Theological Dramatic Theory, IV: The Action*, trans. Graham Harrison (San Francisco: Ignatius, 1994], 95-135). This absence is curious for many reasons, not least because the Bible, the primary textual source for all Christian theology, describes temporality as much in terms of calendars, memorials, and solemn assemblies as it does in terms of abstract concepts or even natural circadian, diurnal, or annual rhythms.

theologians, time is not something human beings form or articulate, but a natural power to which we submit.

Thus far, all too sketchily, the conversations into which I want to insert Rosenstock-Huessy. What does he have to say?

II

In important respects, Rosenstock-Huessy anticipated Giddens and Adam in their critique of sociology's understanding of time, and also anticipated recent theologians' critique of the modern "flattening" of time. He decries the social and psychological effects of modern time:

> We need the intersecting of many rhythms of time. Our stomach and our consciousness respond to a 24-hour rhythm. Our faith and our hopes respond to centuries. Our noble passions like the love of husband and wife, of veterans, of sects, rule time spans of 25, 30, or 40 years. The 24-hour day and the week, the month and the year, should not becloud the spheres of greater revolution. The chronology

---

Leviticus 23 and Deuteronomy 14-16 have played virtually no role in the formulation of recent theologies of time. It is not surprising that the theologians who have given the most concrete attention to temporality have been liturgical theologians. See, for instance, Alexander Schmemann, *For the Life of the World* (Crestwood, NY: St. Vladimir's Seminary Press, 1997), ch. 3.

of family succession, of wars and peaces, has been destroyed by the heresy that the mechanical time clock revealed all there is to be lived in time, by time, and by timing.[19]

At the center of Rosenstock-Huessy's treatment of time is his insight into the multiform character of the present. By emphasizing the *multiformity* of time, Rosenstock-Huessy challenges the two-dimensionality of modern linear time. He reverses the Cartesian privileging of space, arguing that Descartes wrongly "put time into space, made time at its best a fourth dimension of space."[20] Moderns recognize that our lived human spaces are multiform products of the past formed by human art, power, technology, and cultivation. But for modernity, however, time is treated as a simple datum of nature, not a social or human product.[21]

---

19. Eugen Rosenstock-Huessy, "Time-Bettering Days" in *Rosenstock-Huessy Papers, Volume 1* (Norwich, VT: Argo Books, 1954), 16.

20. Quoted in Morgan, *Speech and Society*, 29.

21. Rosenstock-Huessy, "Time-Bettering Days," 4. In an impassioned passage, Rosenstock-Huessy gives the formula for creating modern time: "Count the 24 hours of the day in the abstract over large standardized regions called Eastern, Seaboard, or Mountain Time. Swallow up all the concrete specific empirical observable noon hours when the sun is in his zenith, in favour of the general and theoretical whistle that blows and sends us all scurrying for our sandwiches. Disconnected the precalculated social time from its sensual origins in the sunsets and sunrises and real moonlights at the place of your actual

Rosenstock-Huessy also recognizes that the modern philosophy of temporality is bound up with social and economic factors, which make's modernity's mathematicization and secularization of time far more radical than anything in the ancient world.[22]

Against this, Rosenstock-Huessy insists that the distinctions of past, present and future, and even the present

---

habitation. Disconnected it also from the religious calendars with their "ridiculous" movement of Easter. Better the spaces in which men work, play, live; build bigger and better stadiums. But do not better the times" (Rosenstock-Huessy, "Time-Bettering Days," 3-4).

22. Modernity's regularization of time has some roots in antiquity, in Plato's efforts to subordinate time to the *logos* of number. Plato calculated the proper size of a city's population by conforming it to the celestial calendar: "Every hour and every month some citizen had to observe the worship of the Gods in the sky. Now 12 x 12 equals 144. Plato concluded that his city must have 5040 citizens because 5040 can be divided into 144 by 35 observing crews" (Rosenstock-Huessy, "Time-Bettering Days," 4). This is a city that forbids "private devotions, private teaching, personal lyrics, individual philosophy," as it repeats the "calendar without the slightest change through eternity" (Rosenstock-Huessy, "Time-Bettering Days," 5). Yet, the Platonic regularization of time did not create a secular city. For Plato, "the cosmic order acts as our teacher. . . . And this means that Plato's City is purely educational; teaching the natural order is its highest goal." At the same time, the festivals of the city are set aside so that the citizens could "feast" and "cohabit" with the gods. By turning to the heavens for guidance, "the Platonic City meets the gods halfway. Serious toil is one half of our gate; it represents earth. Dances and songs are the representatives of the Gods." The fault in Plato's system is the dualism inherent in it, a dualism of "earth and heaven," of "toil and orgy," of "stars and streets" (Rosenstock-Huessy, "Time-Bettering Days," 5).

itself, are human artifacts, products of social interactions and especially of speech. From this, Rosenstock-Huessy concludes not only that time is multiform, but specifically that the *present* has a multiform character. Any generation, any moment of history, contains a multitude of "distemporaries" who can be formed into a "contemporary" present only by speech.[23] Teaching provides a paradigm case. Teacher and students do not arrive at the classroom as "contemporaries" but as "distemporaries." The teacher is always "older," at least in his exposure to the material, the student is always "younger" either because he has never been exposed to the material or because he has not been exposed to it so deeply as the teacher.[24] The fact that teaching takes place at all gives hope that time can be synchronized by speech, and old/past and young/future can be harmonized in the time of the classroom, a common "present." Appealing to Augustine's *de Magistro*, Rosenstock-Huessy notes that distemporaries can forge a common present only "if they admit that they form a succession, if they affirm their quality of belonging to different times."[25] This mutual recognition is what forms the present time, and this shows that the "present" is multiform, produced by the imbrication of past and future.

---

23. *Speech and Reality*, 28.

24. Rosenstock-Huessy, "Man Must Teach," 6-9.

25. Rosenstock-Huessy, "Man Must Teach," 8.

At least since Augustine, philosophers have puzzled over the reality-status of the present, that knife-edge between the past that slips away and the future that moves relentlessly forward. For Augustine, the present is the vaporous moment that dies as soon as it lives. Because Rosenstock-Huessy views the articulation of time as a product of human speech, he can make sense of "presents" of varying shapes and sizes, and demonstrate that these are not simply illusions. The "twentieth century" is not a chimera but a coherent epoch, a "body of time" with bulk and shape, and so are more modest "presents" like "dinnertime" and "worship" and "playtime."[26]

Humans create the multiform present in speech and in speech-filled social action. What means do they have for creating contemporaneity? Given the limits of this study, I will examine only three social instruments that, in Rosenstock-Huessy's words, "cut alleys of time" or shape "bodies of time": ritual, holidays, and calendars.

Ritual

Rituals bestow clothing, and according to Rosenstock-Huessy, dress does not simply cover the body but

---

26. His description of the present is in my judgment the most fruitful philosophical insight into the nature of time. It overcomes the subjectivizing tendencies of Augustine's account, and is far superior to Bergson's notion of temporal "emergence."

"replaces" it,[27] giving a new office and identity. What makes humans human is the capacity to take on new dress and new bodies: "this 'many-bodiedness' is the real secret of men. Primeval man felt that he must 'don' the eagle's feathers, the lion's mane and the elephant's proboscis, and thereby temporarily play their roles in society."[28]

Ritual investiture is an instrument for the articulation of time, and this conception of ritual is rooted in Rosenstock-Huessy's grammatical sociology and especially his understanding of the sociology of grammatical moods. As he explains in his early essay, "The Practical Knowledge of the Soul," this view is embodied already in Greek grammar, which makes the "I" the "first person." As he points out, "all our experience teaches us exactly the opposite of this Greek premise, that the single 'I' is primary." A child develops by "gradually stak[ing] out its borders as an independent entity," by siphoning out the "thousand cares, impressions, and influences which surround, flow around, and beset it." What a child first recognizes is not a world, nor father and mother, but "that it is spoken to": "It is smiled at, entreated, rocked, comforted, punished, given presents, or nourished. It is first a 'you' to a powerful being outside itself—above all to its parents." Goethe said that a father is always his daughter's first god; Rosenstock-Huessy

---

27. Rosenstock-Huessy, *Origin of Speech*, 74.

28. *OS*, 75.

agrees, adding that "He is so because he is present for his daughter before her own 'I' is, and because he bestows on her the consciousness of herself, by addressing her as 'you.'" Before we can articulate anything about our own existence, we hear "others say that we exist and mean something to them." Thus, "we develop self-consciousness by receiving commands and being judged from outside. In the face of these commands and judgments, we perceive that we are someone special, and being something different or special is the fundamental experience of the 'I.'"[29] We become Egos in response to commands. Hence, the original mood of our social speech is not the indicative but the imperative.

Indicatives close rather than open cones of time. For Rosenstock-Huessy, the primacy of logic is a grammatical phenomenon, the primacy of the indicative. Since the Greeks, the indicative, in the form of "This is an answer," has dominated logic and philosophy, and through them all forms of thought. Other moods of speech are considered derivative, or are forced to conform to the indicative. But the triumph of the indicative, of "This is an answer," is arbitrary. The Bible, Rosenstock-Huessy suggests, discards this Greek logic entirely. Instead of granting primacy to the indicative, the Bible deals in imperatives, interrogatives, optatives, and narratives. Unlike other moods, the indica-

---

29. "Practical Knowledge of the Soul," 16. For a fuller discussion, see Peter J. Leithart, "Grammar on the Cross," in Wayne Cristaudo, ed., *The Cross and the Star* (Cambridge: Cambridge Scholars Press, 2009).

tive detaches the speaker from the listener and from reality. An indicative does not require the presence of the speaker or the hearer in the way that the other forms of speech do:

> My sentence "he is answering him" is much more specific about my own person than the other: "this is an answer." The pure brain is free to say the latter sentence. The whole man—legs, arms, rump and brain—must exist in the same pace and time for the former. The speaker of the sentence "this is an answer" is an abstract being.[30]

Rituals of investiture are enacted imperatives. They create an epochal break in time because they constitute a break in identity: "The polarity of dress and speech is the polarity of before and after."[31] Dress orients to a new future by marking a social role and commanding the wearer to grow into his role.[32] Investiture thus marks the beginning of a body of time.[33] Naming too is a social and political

---

30. *OS*, 42.

31. *OS*, 79.

32. *OS*, 75.

33. Rosenstock-Huessy rightly rejects the truism of much anthropology and comparative religion that rituals are participations in a timeless Ur-time.

instrument for articulating time: [34] A leader gives "his name to the time of his group," enabling the group to "cooperate in a reasoned and articulate direction."[35] There really is an "age of Louis XIV" or a "Victorian age," which began as a body of time by coronation.

Rituals must impose their imperatives over long periods of time, lest they become ludicrous:

> One cannot afford the ceremonies of an ordination for working one week in a factory. With such an attitude, the wedding ceremony becomes "for better, for divorce," or "from bed to worse." In our historical reality, rituals are everywhere cheapened by increasingly being used for brief stages of life. This process leads to vulgarization and secularization.[36]

---

34. Rosenstock-Huessy writes, "The king who is crowned, the President who is inaugurated, give their name to time. Their reign covers the years with the one name in whose authority all statutes are enacted, all postal stamps and coins printed, and all school children's chronology fixed. The greatest event of any political group is the ceremony by which a "namegiver" is instituted. Long before people had legislators like Moses or Solon, they had name-givers. *Nomos* and *onoma* (order and name), are related terms in many languages for the obvious reason that by their name leaders imparted order to time" (*OS*, 77).

35. *OS*, 77.

36. *OS*, 80. Baptism, Rosenstock-Huessy says, attempts to make itself heard for twenty years, and more: "The great venture of baptism consists in the attempt to speak impressively to this child over his or her

This is a diminution of life, because "man is not human" until he is able to bring physical and social life into some kind of unity. Ritual makes this integration possible, and to do its work it has to connect generations, not weeks or months:

> Ritual is measured in generations; the yardstick of a ritual's perfection is its power to tie together whole generations of men. A ritual that does less is second rate and cannot help us interpret the rituals of primary importance.[37]

Rituals name and dress; memorial ceremonies are, by contrast, indicatives that "record": "To have made a name for yourself means literally to make other people talk and think of you! Through his recorders a person speaks to posterity, to the world."[38] As imperatives, investitures initiate a period of time that ends when the name of the one invested is memorialized or recorded. Time is formed socially as humans press it between the imperative of ritual and the indic-

---

first twenty years. It takes quite some courage to try to make yourself heard over twenty years, but baptism attempts just this. The ceremony performed is meant to form the hearing and to draw the attention and to awaken the understanding of a child over his whole period of growth" (OS, 79-80).

37. OS, 81.

38. OS, 79.

ative of memorialization.[39] Rituals, and the formal speech that goes with them, "cut out alleys of time" that last "thirty or forty years into the future."[40] Rituals form a "present" just as truly as the distemporary teacher and students for a contemporary moment in the classroom. "This present exists nowhere in nature," Rosenstock-Huessy writes, "but we can create it by uniting in a name and by pooling our diverse lifetimes into one great reservoir of supper time."[41] Rituals thus articulate a multiform present.

Holidays

In Rosenstock-Huessy's view, Shakespeare's phrase "Time-Bettering Days" (Sonnet 82) is "the most radical faith in progress in any linguistic expression known to me." Shakespeare hints that "time which is the totality and compound of all days [may] be improved by days which are better than the rest."[42] Holidays, Rosenstock-Huessy argues, are "time-bettering days," days that improve time.

----

39. Though to my knowledge Rosenstock-Huessy never makes the connection, it seems consistent with his thought to suggest that "bodies of time" mimic the shape of human history as a whole. In a biblical framework, history begins with the ritualized imperatives of creation, and ends with the memorialized indicatives of the final judgment.

40. *OS*, 81.

41. *OS*, 81.

42. Rosenstock-Huessy, "Time-Bettering Days," 1-2.

How? Holidays better time by furthering communities, forming a group with something "common":

> On a holiday, we share one time and one space although we are divided by self-interest, by age, by wealth, by occupation, by climate, by language, by race, by history; we carry one as though we were one and the same man, regardless of birth, unafraid of death, unabashed by sex, unperturbed by fear.[43]

Even the apparent idleness of a Puritan town was productive because it was a matter of being idle *together*: "The Puritans were terribly busy and went to great expense to labor for being idle together. The gathering of the idle was primary."[44]

Like much of the earlier Western experience and accounting of time, the holiday has fallen by the wayside: "We no longer can select new Time-bettering Days with conviction. Modern Christmas and even more Mother's Day, Father's Day, have become business-bettering days. They certainly do not better the times."[45] With the rise of the factory system, we began to lose the "recipe" for building communities: "The power of building a city is taken

---

43. Rosenstock-Huessy, *CF*, 199.

44. *CF*, 204.

45. Rosenstock-Huessy, "Time-Bettering Days," 17.

away from those who have 'un-learned' how to celebrate a holiday together."

Instead of holidays, we have leisure. The two are not the same. "Leisure is . . . a 'too much' or a surplus of individual time while holidays are rooted in a tragedy for the whole community. On holidays, a community triumphs over tragedy; a man at leisure idles away his time."[46] Leisure is always a movement "away from the center of existence to some outlying district." Leisure can flit from one pole to another on the Cross of Reality,[47] but at each pole it lacks seriousness because it refuses to "stick to man's true place in the middle of the Cross."[48] Leisure is individualized idleness, replacing the communal and community-building idleness of the holiday: "being at leisure with others is accidental and arbitrary, and therefore the communion does

---

46. *CF*, 199.

47. Rosenstock-Huessy writes, "The man at leisure, trying to get away from himself, may go before himself into the past, after himself into the future; he may penetrate into the inner core or look around in the external world." A man may spend his leisure in exploring the outside world in travel and sight-seeing, becoming a kind of seducer of, a "mental Don Juan of irresponsible conquest," since both the globe-trotter and the seducer are aroused to curiosity by the "secrets of something outside of us, separate in nature" (*CF*, 201). Many moderns spend their leisure "in a kind of constant dutiful shift from backward to forward to inward to outward entertainment; like a man on his sickbed, many souls roll from one direction to the other since they do not understand the rhythm and flee the center of their lives."

48. *CF*, 201.

not reach into the depth of the leisure. Leisure isolates the soul."[49] Leisure is not "time-bettering" because it does not enrich the socially formed time of a community.

Holidays, by contrast, place us at the center of existence where death becomes the gate to life. When Rosenstock-Huessy says that a community triumphs over tragedy in holiday, he means, in part, that holidays commemorate the great moments, often the great crises, of a community's history. Not everything that happened at the fall of the Bastille, or during the Revolution that followed, was happy; but in celebrating Bastille Day, France affirms its survival beyond the tragedy. In fact, it celebrates more than survival: Through the holiday the tragic events, the death involved in the events commemorated, are incorporated into communal life, as we look "with 'condescension' . . . on our conflicts because we have triumphed over them, and we find in the victory over tragic conflict the deepest meaning of our destiny." When we observe holidays,

> the soul becomes whole. She accepts her many weekday conflicts or trends because she no longer has to fear them as curses but may accept them as her wealth. She may do so because she proves to herself, on the holiday, her ultimate freedom from

49. *CF*, 204.

every one of them, by communion, by fellowship. Holidays are the mortar of society.[50]

When we view the painful events of the past on a holiday of the holiday, "we see the connection of death with birth, of darkness with light, of heaven with earth."[51]

---

50. *CF*, 202. Somewhat more fully, he writes, "the community needs for its own health a holiday. On this holiday [after the World War], the tragedy of losses in battles is not forgotten as when we are trying to take our minds off something disagreeable. The power of a holiday consists in the ascendancy over tragedy. No holiday without pain remembered and suffered sanctified. From this bravery higher certainty of our true calling is acquired. Any army which comes home furnishes the community with the "natural" experience of a holiday. In it, our life is restored to the full stature of its strength because in pain, in disgrace, in desperation, the holiday is rooted; but its fruits are the rebirth of the community" (*CF*, 214).

51. *CF*, 214-15. Rosenstock-Huessy believes that the de-rhythmization of modern life, especially in factories, is one of the social pre-conditions for the rise of psychoanalysis: "Psychoanalysis is the obvious reaction to this deeper lack of rhythm which factory and suburb imposed on us. The knots of personal time are untied by the analyst in an individualistic fashion. But even the doctors themselves are becoming aware of the deficiency of their method. The fellowship of a normal group, not the hothouse of sick individual consciences, is the answer to our hunger for rhythm" (*CF*, 211). Without holidays, humans are deprived of a necessary rhythm of time, and suffer psychologically. The political consequences of the collapse of the holiday are equally drastic. It is not merely, Rosenstock-Huessy argues, that we lose a sense of "togetherness." If we do not discover a common time-and-space in the holiday, the result will be world war: "Western industrial society did not produce this week, year, or this holiday in

Calendars

As his letters to Rosenzweig reveal, Rosenstock-Huessy was obsessed with calendars from an earlier age, and he retained that obsession throughout his academic career. The development of a calendar is a cultivation of memory: "A day introduced into the calendar or a day stricken out of the calendar, means a real change in the education and tradition of a nation." Calendars are thus a form of history-writing:

> Mankind writes its own history long before the historians visit its battlefields; days, festivals, holidays, the order of meals, rest and vacations, together with religiously observed rituals and symbols, are sources of political history, though rarely used by the average political or economic historian.[52]

Calendars reveal history as the "autobiography" of a people, and ultimately the unified autobiography of the entire human race. According to Rosenstock, mankind would lack autobiography if human society had "always been like

time. And so, the World Wars came instead." The experiences that are given in holiday—communion in a common task—were created by the wars, which gave opportunity "for millions" to "leave their insipid existence and have these very experiences" (*CF*, 214). Holidays are opportunities for kind of common experience and common task and thus provide part of a "moral equivalent of war."

52. *Out of Revolution*, 8.

modern society: completely sensational, totally forgetful, and wonderfully devoid of memory." But man has not always been so. Rather, "mankind has always, with the utmost tenacity, cultivated its calendar." [53]

Like ritual, calendars are a social and political instrument for cutting alleys of time.[54] Calendars shape time in two senses. First, the cataclysmic events commemorated on calendars are products of political and social action, and these events open or close epochs, just as rituals of investiture and commemoration open and close alleys of time. Second, it is not merely the events themselves that give form to time, but the creative social decision to mark events on the calendar. As Tolstoy knew, as a historical event the Battle of Waterloo was a slather of blood and slaughter, too complex for any individual in the battle to know what it was all about. Waterloo "became a name, an impression, and a reality long before the historians sat down to write of it." The name was assigned to highlight the fact that some

---

53. *Out of Revolution*, 8.

54. The significance of a change in the calendar is not always immediately evident, and may not be evident for several generations. Still, nations mark days as a bride marks her wedding day as the day of new creation: "It is not necessary to record the everyday life of a nation for a thousand years in order to know its aim and inspiration. The great creations of history do not reveal their deepest sense nor their soul every day. But each has its wedding day; and the words and songs, the promises and laws of this period of a nation's life express its character viva voce and settle its destiny once and for all" (*Out of Revolution*, 9).

features, some actions, some human traits, tower above the mire of incomprehensible sufferings and hardships as the individual tradition of this particular victory and defeat."

Similarly, "Gettysburg, Saratoga, Yorktown, Marathon, are not facts but the creations of a nation's memory." These events are named as towering events in a nation's autobiography by being marked on the calendar.[55]

By emphasizing the importance of calendars, Rosenstock-Huessy is developing his insight that national memory is not built by scientific history or by literature, because "it is not an effort of the intellect." Instead, "The whole being of the nation is at stake in a great event," and this experience can only be memorialized in more formal ways, through monuments and ceremonies. At the end of this process, "The climax is reached when an event is incorporated into the calendar as a recurrent date. Memory is fixed by the calendar of a group or a nation." A day of memorial for Becket was added to the calendar, identifying him as a martyr of the church by putting his day on a day earlier reserved for King David, immediately after the day of St. Stephen. This occurred only two years after Becket's death, and this dating "under the authority of the Pope in Rome, tells us more about the mediaeval relations between Gregorian Rome and a local kingdom than do many discussions of the Anglicans during the nineteenth century." The day

---

55. *Out of Revolution*, 693-694.

of Thomas was "the 'Fourteenth of July' of the Papal Revolution, and the Magna Charta of the common man from 1174-1535."[56]

Rosenstock-Huessy intended his use of calendrical evidence to provoke a revolution in historiography. Because calendars represent a social formation of time, attention to calendars makes for more accurate accounting of the periods of history. Rosenstock-Huessy complains that "Periods like that of Humanism or of the Industrial Revolution are afterthoughts, not born of original, contemporary experience." Far more candid are "the historical calendars built up immediately in the way of revolutions." Secondary periodizations like "Renaissance" or "Industrial Revolution" "should not be allowed to dominate the Great Year of mankind as it is pictured in the creations of real holidays and traditions by monks, papacy, free cities, princes, parliaments, citizens and workers."[57]

Calendars also capture the rhythmic character of "all religions," which "aspire to rhythmical activities." Rosenstock-Huessy argues that "dance is sanctified; religious dance recommended; and dancing is rhythm on a short wave." In the church, "we have liturgical movement to revive the rhythm of the individual service and of the whole year of the Church as well. Sermons grown into contin-

---

56. *Out of Revolution*, 694-695.

57. *Out of Revolution*, 705.

uous chains over months and even years." Calendars en-
shrine this rhythmic character of religion: "Calendars are
rhythmical forms of memory and cycles of worship. The liturgical rhythm is expressed in terms of Sunday and weekday, Christmas and Easter, Pentecost and Advent."[58] These
rhythms are not identical to the rhythms of nature, and the
church's calendar in particular defies natural time:

> The former is a calendar of 365 days. The latter ex-
> presses within the scope of 365 days the true infin-
> ity of all time from beginning of the world to its
> end. For the reasoning mind, time consists of sep-
> arate units, days or years. For our faith, one year's
> course inducts into the whole linear expanse of all
> history. The calendar of the Western World, with its

---

58. *CF*, 207. Philosophical systems are not rhythmical, but religions
are. Religion is closer to life in this respect, in that life itself expresses
itself in the rhythm of the "mutual begetting of opposites: weeping
and joy, winter and summer, victory and defeat, birth and death,
make up the rhythm." Religion mimics this with a pattern of Sunday
and weekday (*CF*, 208). Yet, religion does not imitate the rhythms of
nature. Nature is rhythmic, but "our time rhythm is unhinged from
the solar revolutions." Human sexual rhythms are different from the
cycles of the animal world: "Whales and horses may take their law of
mating from the seasons. The human is made miserable because his
appetites are unpredictable. Sex, politics, studies, work, and especially
our worries and anxieties, make us exiles from the annual cycle Man
as exile from nature's cycles, perpetually creates new rhythms" (*CF*,
209).

Fourth of July, is independent from nature's mechanism. So much so, that from Christmas to Easter, a whole lifetime of thirty years is remembered, and from Pentecost to Advent, the whole experience of mankind through the Old Testament and our whole era is remembered.[59]

Calendars are, thus, a uniquely social articulation of time. They are created by nations and peoples, and they give shape to time in a way that obviously does not simply reproduce the patterns of natural time.

III

Though Rosenstock-Huessy frequently speaks the language of sociology, his understanding of time is deeply animated by Christian convictions concerning Jesus, His death and resurrection, and eschatology.[60] For Rosenstock-Huessy,

---

59. *CF*, 209.

60. I can't enter fully into the debate about Rosenstock-Huessy's relation to orthodox Christianity. I read him as a "revolutionary orthodox Christian." For the moment, I support that with two small pieces of evidence. First, Rosenstock-Huessy explicitly claims to be Christo- and cruci-centric: "The Crucifixion is the fountainhead of all my values" (*CF*, 102). Second, he claimed to have concluded at a young age that the Nicene Creed was obvious (see Wayne Cristaudo, "Eugen Rosenstock-Huessy," *Stanford Encyclopedia of Philosophy*, available at http://plato.stanford.edu/entries/rosenstock-huessy). Cristaudo argues that Rosenstock-Huessy articulated a "Christianity

Christianity gives unity to humanity's times by giving humanity a common future. Without this religious impulse, Rosenstock-Huessy's emphasis on the social articulation of time could easily lend itself to tribalism, as each human group articulates time with its own rituals, calendars, and holidays. Humanity lives a unified time and history only because of Jesus.[61]

The unity of times is a central theme of the Christian gospel. Rosenstock-Huessy attacks modern New Testament scholarship for making Jesus a creature of His time. On the contrary, the gospel announces that "the Breath of a new Spirit was breathed and it enthroned the Master who would initiate as well as subscribe eras, and out of whose mouth the beginnings and ends of all the eras would be

---

of non-transcendence." I find that claim overstated, but even if that is true, it does not necessarily undermine the argument that Rosenstock-Huessy was an orthodox Christian. There are, after all, different ways of construing "transcendence," some of which are incompatible with the Christian confession of *creatio ex nihilo*. M. Darrol Bryant ("The Grammar of the Spirit: Time, Speech and Society," in Bryant and Hans Huessy, eds., *Eugen Rosenstock-Huessy: Studies in His Life and Thought* [Lewiston, NY: Edwin Mellen, 1986], 233-260) is in my view entirely correct in finding the unity of Rosenstock-Huessy's work in his robust, if eccentric, Christian faith, and Bryant's is also the best treatment of Rosenstock-Huessy's understanding of time that I have found.

61. There are a number of important themes in Rosenstock-Huessy's work that I cannot treat here, most importantly his notion of a Johannine age of Christianity.

interpreted and understood."[62] Christ is not the creature of time, but time's master, who inaugurates the Christian era and whose word renews and re-renews throughout that era. Only because the Word became flesh is it possible to overcome the Babel of tongues and the confusion of times that results from the variety of speech.[63]

Though all religions lend rhythm to time, Christianity's achievement is unique since "mankind in the Christian era lives in a pluralism of intersecting and overlapping calendars" and "this is the distinction of the Christian era against all others, Jewish, Chinese, Roman, Aztec and all the rest." The Christian era is "the era of pluralism in timing, and this is officially its character." Since Jesus "the Lord of the Eons of Eons has become flesh," time has "been allowed to become a spectrum just as waves or colors." This, Rosenstock-Huessy says, is the "fullness of time bestowed upon us in this eon."[64]

Rosenstock-Huessy expounds on the "fullness" of the Christian era by pointing to the complexity of time in Western civilization. Despite the triumph of capitalist rationalization, Cartesian philosophy, and Newtonian science, Rosenstock-Huessy finds remnants of Christian tem-

---

62. Rosenstock-Huessy, *The Fruit of Our Lips*, xviii.

63. Stahmer, "Christianity in the Early Writings of Eugen Rosenstock-Huessy," in Bryant and Huessy, *Eugen Rosenstock-Huessy*, 37-38.

64. Rosenstock-Huessy, "Time-Bettering Days," 1.

poral fullness in the academic calendar, which refuses to follow the business calendar. Schools are in session for only nine months of the year, and give students time off during the "Winter Carnival." This winter recess shows that for the academic world, "holidays determine spaces," since "everybody goes home. The individual student is sucked back into the place of his own nativity. The people who surround him at Christmas are his pre-academics. . . . At the winter solstice his past rises once more to swallow him up." Commencement also gives the academic year a freedom that the business calendar lacks, freeing students for three months to pursue their own desires—to work in any number of settings, travel, play.[65] However Platonic the inspiration behind the liberal arts college, its calendar is a Christian creation, and it is indebted to the "complex inheritance of the ecclesiastical polity." Colleges embody "one element" of the earlier Christian calendar: "a body of time lived not for a livelihood, not lived for a standard of living, not lived for good works or for work or for service; no, a body of time lived under the expectation of the novice, under the promise of the experienced, under the pressure of fruitfulness." In short, "The college calendar, more and more, is the bulwark of free time against factory time. Therefore it is a religious institution of Christianity."[66]

---

65. Rosenstock-Huessy, "Time-Bettering Days," 7.

66. Rosenstock-Huessy, "Time-Bettering Days," 9. At the same time,

The college calendar is the remnant of what was once a "great way of heavenly life on earth."[67] Times for medieval Christians were intertwined symbolically. The day had to have twelve hours because the day was the image of the year

---

Rosenstock-Huessy recognizes that certain orderings of time, including the college calendar, can fragment humanity and break social bonds. Students who operate by the college calendar have little sense of the time of factory workers or farmers. Rosenstock-Huessy's acute awareness of the problem led him to create Camp William James, an effort to brings students, farmers, and workers together in adult education.

67. Rosenstock-Huessy blames radical Protestants for the destruction of Christian time: "Nobody more than the Puritans murdered the whole church calendar and emasculated it so as to consist of 52 sabbaths" (Rosenstock-Huessy, "Time-Bettering Days," 9). For earlier Christians, however, time was variable, and small periods of time could be taken as representations of larger periods of time, thus filling days and years with epochs. Medievals, Rosenstock-Huessy claims, "did not live abstractly," and thus the "twelve" hours of the day were not constant spans of time. Medieval people followed the actual patterns of the days: "at the two solstices, the twelve hours though still twelve, had a very different content. On a June 21st, sunrise might come at 4 in the morning, sunset at 8 in the evening. In that case, 16 times 60 minutes were to be divided by 12 as there always were to be 12 hours. Hence each hour 80 minutes long. On December 21, with a day of perhaps 8 hours of sunlight, the single hour was composed of 40 minutes only." Moderns ignore these variations: "We moderns command the sun and moon by our standardized regional abstract times. We violate experience by our mental tyranny." All the time, we claim to be following the course of natural time, when in fact "we are interested in conventions" (Rosenstock-Huessy, "Time-Bettering Days," 11).

of twelve months. And for the medieval monks, days and weeks were images of the whole of eternity: "The canonical hours of one day aptly represented the 7-day week. Prime at sunrise, terce, sixth, none, vesper and compline divided every day of the monk's life into the whole cycle of all times. The sun's day represented the week: the light was his Sabbath, and her laudes in the dark. Correspondingly the week had 7 days, the world 7 ages." Thus, "Praying 7 times a day also meant to daily live through the Seven Days of the Great Week of Easter, and since the Great Week of Easter is the Queen of all the other 51 weeks, indirectly one single day was lived in the light of all times." For medievals, time "was not a quantity, but a melody."[68] And it was a melody that rose to a closing crescendo. In contrast to other calendars, which trace time as it "rushed downhill eagerly from the meaningful five days of the New Year," the Christian calendar stretches *forward* eschatologically to the celebration of Easter and Pentecost.[69] It is at once evident that Ro-

---

68. Rosenstock-Huessy, "Time-Bettering Days," 12.

69. Rosenstock-Huessy, "Time-Bettering Days," 12-13. The loss of this richly melodious time is also a loss of speech, specifically a loss of metaphor. Moderns have, he says, "lost this immediate power to accept a particle as the representative of a whole," and as a result 'most of the language of Church and Synagogue, of antiquity, is lost to us." We reduce expressions like "God's hand" as "mere metaphors," forgetful that our finger "only got its name from its quality of there also being God's finger, and the Day only was observed because it stood for eternity" (Rosenstock-Huessy, "Time-Bettering Days," 13).

senstock-Huessy's discussion is far more concrete, far more *sociological*, than many theological treatments of time, but it is equally clear that this is no immanent account of time. Rosenstock-Huessy instead offers an integrated social theology of time or theology of social time.

He integrates sociological and theological accounts also in his treatment of the once-for-all character of Jesus' work. Once-for-all events are central to Rosenstock-Huessy's vision of history. Like investiture rituals, catastrophes and momentous events open up a body of time that can extend for centuries. Luther is unique, once-for-all, and yet within a generation the world is filled with imitators, who identify themselves as "Lutherans" and over time the Lutheran spirit fills even those who no longer adhere to Luther's own doctrine.

Though once-for-all events happen periodically in history, for Rosenstock-Huessy the complex event of Jesus' cross-and-resurrection is the once-for-all event of all once-for-all events, the source for recurring deaths and resurrections in individual life and in civilization. Jesus opens up a final epoch that is the last of all epochs because it is fullness of epochs: "crucifixion (or last judgment) and resurrection would not be known as everyday occurrences in our lives if they had not happened once for all, with terrific majesty."[70] Jesus plants the seed of death-and-resurrection,

---

70. *CF*, 103-104.

and this bears fruit repeatedly in moments of transforming anguish. As the Crucified and Risen Man, Jesus creates a new form of humanity, a new style of human being and of being human in community. He is not merely a man among men, but "the norm, the way, the truth, and the life to be developed by us beyond the state in which we find ourselves." He is "my maker" because He is the first man "who was neither Greek nor Jew nor Scythe, but complete and perfect humanity, and each of the rest of us, if we are not simply jealous like Nietzsche, must be content with being his men."[71] As the new man, Jesus brings in the fullness of humanity and of humanity's times, and because of His once-for-all death and resurrection, He injects into time the power to remake times. Through His death and resurrection, Jesus brings the fullness of time that is the power of the future. Here Rosenstock-Huessy offers a thoroughly Christological "theology of social time."

On the rare occasions when he deals with time in Trinitarian terms, Rosenstock-Huessy unites sociological concerns with orthodox theological formula. He appeals to the Western doctrine of the "double procession" of the Spirit to suggest a Trinitarian account of time. Were a single generation to occupy the earth by itself, it would need "no religion," especially not a religion "which talks of Father

71. *CF*, 104.

and Son as equally responsible for the spirit." The Western Trinitarian formula, however,

> connotes some process which runs counter to the spirit of any one generation. . . . In the Divinity, Father and Son unfold the quality of being, by spreading it over two generations. And the Spirit, lest he be confused with the wit of the moment, is explicitly said to descend from the interaction of the two generations, the Father and the Son.

So also humanity "can't be the image of God if he serves the spirit of his own time."[72] Teaching again becomes a paradigm example. Liberalism captures some of the Christian spirit in its effort to educate children to reach "a future from which the parents themselves were excluded."[73] Liberal education has failed insofar as it has failed to imitate the Triune life. Instead of the classroom spirit being the unified product of the procession of the spirit of the father and the spirit of the son, it is turned into a purely contemporaneous event. Instead of striving to unite "two ages," "teachers and students on our campuses lived under the fiction that they were contemporaries and could

---

72. *CF*, 219-20.

73. *CF*, 225.

feel and think the same things."[74] The spirit of the age thus becomes an unbalanced "spirit of the sons," rather than a spirit of the "fathers and the sons."

Rosenstock-Huessy's analysis of the time of teaching provides a final example of the integration of theological and sociological perspectives. Teachers, as noted above, are "old" in comparison to the students, and to become old is a form of dying, a death to possibilities and plasticities that are still open options for the young. To become old is to be acquainted with death, to become increasingly fixed and formed. A teacher renounces his youthful play for the sake of his students, and as a result he always seems older to his students than he really is. In return for this renunciation, he is allowed to reach past his own death and affect a future that he will never enter: "Man . . . wants to determine the future. One form of determining the future is teaching."[75] This "forwardizing force" is the driving force of teaching, a force that Rosenstock-Huessy also links with love. Students, on the other hand, are driven by a "backwardizing" force, which Rosenstock-Huessy identifies with faith. Teachers throw out a "feeler" to the future, students a feeler to the past. When forwardizing teachers and backwardizing students come together, they form a "body of time," a socially formed present.

---

74. *CF*, 225.

75. Rosenstock-Huessy, "Man Must Teach," 30.

This present is not only the product of the social action of teaching but more fundamentally a product of the exercise of the theological virtues. It cannot come to expression without the operation of what Rosenstock-Huessy calls the "social energies" of faith, hope and love:

> The past means a before-my-time background, to be conquered by faith. The future means an after-my-life-time to be conquered by love. The timeless present is based on the common hopes of distemporaries that by pooling their time sense, they might become contemporaries of one standstill-present.[76]

In the absence of faith, hope, and love, the future and past haunt us with fears. Psychoanalysis fills us with dread of the consequences of our childhood, while the formless future—nuclear war, or environmental catastrophe—is terrifying. Only through faith, hope, and love, united in teaching and learning in the socially articulated present, is time conquered. Thus, the two themes of "multiformity of the present" and the "fullness of times" come together, since for Rosenstock-Huessy Christian time is uniquely multiform, uniquely a present filled with the promise of the future.

---

76. Rosenstock-Huessy, "Man Must Teach," 35-36.

IV

To clarify how Rosenstock-Huessy's treatment of time enriches both social theory and theology, it is useful to place his work into conversation with a representative of each. As noted above, the social theorist Norbert Elias, best known for his work on the "civilizing process," was a sharp critic of sociology's misconstruals of time. He deplores the "conventional tendency to explore 'nature' and 'society' and, therefore, the physical and sociological problems of 'time' as if they were completely independent of each other," and complains that "to date, enquiries into the sociology of time are almost non-existent."[77] Like Rosenstock-Huessy, he recognizes that time periods (or "presents") are socially formed, and noted that once they are formed, they are treated as natural: "One does not see clearly that a year has a social function and a social reality related to, but distant from, a natural reality; one is apt to perceive it simply as something established by nature."[78] Also like Rosenstock-Huessy, Elias stresses that time is multidimensional.[79]

Elias also recognizes that the "present" is a social creation. Addressing the Augustinian paradox of the evaporating present, he argued that the concept of present is impossible without a concept of past. To speak of a "present"

----

77. Elias, *An Essay on Time,* 38.

78. Elias, *Essay,* 46.

79. Elias, *Essay,* 59.

requires that a group can "distinguish as the present what they are doing here and now, what they are directly experiencing and feeling, both from what is over and subsists only in memory, and from what they may possibly do, experience or suffer, that is, from the past and the future." Past, present, and future are identified in nature only "by virtue of an anthropomorphic identification—that is, figuratively, as when we speak of the future of the sun." In itself, nature is "a continuous sequence of changes in the configurations of energy-matter" so that outside the experiential relationship to human beings, "the division of 'natural' continua of changes into past, present and future is meaningless."[80]

Yet at this point Elias falls back into the very dualism he was contesting. He suggests that the present between two dates "take[s] on the character of the present in conjunction with the experience of a past and a future. In the flow of events there are no segments of this kind. What is past merges seamlessly with the present, as the present does with the future."[81] Rosenstock-Huessy would agree that past, present, and future only make sense, as Elias says, "in human experience,"[82] but Elias takes a subjective, psychological turn when he argues that events are not themselves

---

80. Elias, *Essay*, 64-66.

81. Elias, *Essay*, 67.

82. Elias, *Essay*, 67.

segmented but seamless. For Elias, time has articulation only because of the emergence in the universe "in addition to the four dimensions of space and time, a fifth dimension of consciousness, experience, or however one may express it."[83] Past, present, and future are creations of human consciousness, not of human social activity, of speech. The time of human events, the time of history, is like a natural force to which human beings simply submit but which we do not form. A similar collapse into dualism appears in his brief discussion of early modern science. Galileo, Elias argued, was the first to use time-keeping for other than a social function and that by timing purely "natural" processes (a ball rolling down an inclined plane, for instance) helped to break off natural time from social time.[84] But this is to forget that science is also a social institution.

Rosenstock-Huessy avoids the dualism of which Adam and Elias complain because he recognizes that presents, once articulated by ritual, speech, or events, become objective realities. They do not exist in nature, but they are not simply subjective projections onto a seamless flow of events. Rituals of investiture are, as we have seen, imperatives that initiate a new identity and new direction in the life of an individual, and because the invested individuals are kings, priests, and presidents, their initiation becomes

---

83. Elias, *Essay*, 67.

84. Elias, *Essay*, 85-86.

a seam in the history of a people, or of the world. Ceremonies of commemoration, on the other hand, are indicatives that declare "what happened," and thus close off an alley of time. By these sorts of social actions, "presents" are formed, presents whose multiform character is fully recognized only when it is recognized that human action creates seams in the flow of events.

If Rosenstock-Huessy's differences from Elias arise from his deeper appreciation of the social articulation of the multiform present, his differences from theologians of time arise from his sociological understanding of the evangelical announcement of the "fullness of times." We can clarify his contribution to theologies of time by comparing Rosenstock-Huessy's work with that of Robert Jenson.

For Jenson, the triune name is "simply the biblical account in drastic summary, construed as an account of God's own reality," that is, the biblical account of God's actions in history. In contrast to all Hellenistic religion ("and irreligion," Jenson nicely adds), Christians say that the story of the Bible is really true of God Himself, that He is not motionlessly impassible. Theology does not move from the story to some un-narrated ontological depth. God identifies Himself with and by His story.[85] If this is so, "then

---

85. Robert W. Jenson, "What Is the Point of Trinitarian Theology?" in Christoph Schwöbel, ed., *Trinitarian Theology Today: Essays on Divine Being and Act* (Edinburgh: T&T Clark, 1995), 37. At a number of levels Jenson has affinities with Rosenstock-Huessy, yet Jenson's

God's eternity cannot be the simple absence of time. Then God's eternity must be for him something like what time is for us." Religion, he suggests, is "the cultivation of eternity," eternity understood here as whatever it is that joins the poles of time "to knit future and past into a coherent fabric." Eternity is inherent in every human action; with every action we are attempting to bracket moments to "rhyme remembrance and anticipation into lived present meaning." The question for a religion, though, is how God is eternal. Eternity need not simply be the negation of time; even tribes that look to ancestors do not believe that eternity is simply the evacuation of time. He summarizes this point by saying that the Bible tells a story about God, tells it in a way that we cannot transcend the story and attempt to get at a "real" God without saying the story is false, presents a story with three agents, and tells the story in which each agent is identified by self-distinction from the others.[86]

This leads Jenson to this formulation:
Christ refers all homage from himself to the one who "sent" him, to his "Father," just so accomplishing our salvation and appearing as the Son. This God is the Father only as the one so addressed by

---

abhorrence of the "unbaptized God" would probably extend to an abhorrence of Rosenstock-Huessy's Johannine Age, and the anonymous Christianity that attends it.

86. Jenson, *Trinitarian Theology Today*, 37-38.

the Son; and he then appears in the story centrally as he turns over divine rule to the Son and indeed at the cross "abandons" his role as God, leaving the Son to suffer the consequences of godhead by himself. And the Spirit glorifies as God and testifies to as God the Father or the Son, exactly so enabling the proposition "God is Spirit." [87]

In a move that would have appealed to Rosenstock-Huessy, Jenson relates the persons to grammatical tenses. The Father is the "whence" of every divine event, the Spirit is the "whither," the "divine self-transcendence, insofar as God does not depend upon what is not God to be the referent or energy of this coming to himself. The 'whither' of divine events is not their passive aiming point, but their agent in this mode." He suggests that in addition to processions the church must also talk about the "liberations" of Father and Son as "constitutive of the identity and reality of God."[88]

Also like Rosenstock-Huessy, Jenson highlights the priority of the future, appealing to narrative structure to make his point. Stories are ordered by outcomes, and the story is "a power of the future to liberate each successive specious present from mere predictabilities, from being the

---

87. Jenson, *Trinitarian Theology Today*, 38.

88. Jenson, *Trinitarian Theology Today*, 39.

mere consequences of what has gone before." He asks, "Is there such causation in God? Is his life in straightforward fact ordered by an Outcome which is his outcome, and so in a freedom that is more than abstract aseity? The theology of Mediterranean antiquity thought there could be no such causality in God; the gospel much teach us that there is." Jenson says the Spirit is the specific locus of this liberation: "The Spirit is God as the Power of his own and our future; and it is that the Spirit is God as the Power of his own future, as the Power of a future that is truly 'unexpected' and yet connected, also for him, that the Spirit is a distinct identity of and in God." This is one way that Trinitarian theology "says how God has time, and how God's life is like a good play according to Aristotle."[89]

All this resonates with themes in Rosenstock-Huessy, but what is lacking in Jenson is a concretely "sociological" account of what this theology of time has to do with actual, lived human time, the time of clocks and calendars and rituals. Time remains disembodied; Jenson has no *bodies* of time. In part, the differences between Rosenstock-Huessy and Jenson are a matter of academic specialty. Rosenstock-Huessy was a social philosopher, not a theologian, and his research and writing naturally gravitated toward concrete historical realities.

---

89. Jenson, *Trinitarian Theology Today*, 40–41.

Behind his social philosophy is a theological insight. Elias, with many social scientists, treats time and the "flow of events" as a power beyond human control, and theologians like Jenson likewise often insist time is formed by God, not man. Rosenstock-Huessy does not disagree; Jesus is the master of the times, and the Spirit is the Spirit who unites fathers and sons in the contemporaneity that is human society. Yet, unlike most Christian thinkers, Rosenstock-Huessy does not see the articulation of time as a zero-sum affair, where God's role has to be at the expense of creative human action. At the heart of Rosenstock-Huessy's social theology of time is what he describes as the creedal and patristic idea of anthropurgy, of man-making.[90] The third article of the creed, he says, expresses the Christian notion that by the Spirit humanity is caught up in the process of its own creation.

Rosenstock-Huessy's claims about human formation of time can sound like some overblown version of theosis, but it is important to recognize that the human formation of time that he is talking about is evident everyday in the classroom and the coffee shop, in the formation of calendars and the performance of rituals. It is in the concrete historical experience of nations that human beings are made, that human beings make time. Time makes humanity, and it takes time for God to make humanity; humanity makes

---

90. Rosenstock-Huessy, *Christian Future*.

and indeed makes the time that makes humanity itself; but this human social articulation of time is productive of genuine community only through the exercise of the "social energies" of faith, hope, and love.

V

Much of Rosenstock-Huessy's specific work on calendars, the history of time-keeping, holidays, and rites overlaps with, and has been corrected and expanded by, contemporary sociologists, though few social thinkers display anything close to Rosenstock-Huessy's erudition or energy or expressiveness. His most dramatic contribution to social theory, however, lies in the central place he gives to temporality in his social thought. Social being is being in time because it is being in speech, and vice versa. Long before Giddens complained about sociology's tendency to ignore time, Rosenstock-Huessy had constructed a foundationally temporal social theory. More specifically, Rosenstock-Huessy's recognition that the multiform present is a social creation overcomes the dualisms of social and natural time more effectively than Elias and others. Theologians will benefit from examining the way that Rosenstock-Huessy integrates a specifically theological, specifically Christian, specifically evangelical, account of time (rooted in incarnation, crucifixion, resurrection, and eschatology) with a concrete social account of how Christ brings in the fullness of times. Both social theory and theology would benefit from attention to a thinker equally at home in sociology and theology, equally fascinated by God and clocks.

CHAPTER FIVE

STASIS AND ERUPTION: EUGEN ROSENSTOCK-HUESSY AS A PHILOSOPHER OF 'EVENT'

In modern theology, "apocalyptic" refers to a literary genre characterized by a narrative framework, angelic messengers, and secret revelations. Apocalyptic revelations disclose "a transcendent reality which is both temporal, insofar as it envisages eschatological salvation, and spatial insofar as it involves another, supernatural world."[1] The message is often an eschatological one, the announcement of the world's

---

1. John J Collins, *The Apocalyptic Imagination: An Introduction to Jewish Apocalyptic Literature,* 2nd ed. (Grand Rapids: Eerdmans, 1998), 5.

end, and apocalyptic writings and their associated hopes have often given rise to social movements dedicated to anticipating, speeding, or realizing the promised end.[2]

Since the apocalypse of World War I, the scope of apocalyptic in theology has broadened, as "young, brilliant, brash, and no doubt highly ambitious" theologians began to brandish their "exceedingly paradoxical" apocalyptic theologies to purge the ills of modern culture and theology.[3] In theologians like Karl Barth and Rudolf Bultmann, apocalypse was more than a genre, and had little to do with myths about the end of the physical universe. In Ernst Kasemann's phrase, it was "the mother of all Christian theology."[4] Apocalyptic has proven particularly useful for radical theologians, who, following the lead of Kierkegaard, are dedicated to upsetting the easy accommodations of liberal theology. "Developing the critique of bourgeois, liberal religion in Nietzsche, Kierkegaard, and Overbeck, they transformed the Protestant rejection of the *theologia gloriae* into a virtual mysticism, profoundly resistant to ev-

---

2. cf. Norman Cohn, *The Pursuit of the Millennium: Revolutionary Millenarians and Mystical Anarchists of the Middle Ages* (Oxford: Oxford University Press, 1970).

3. Joshua B. Davis and Douglas Harink, *Apocalyptic and the Future of Theology: With and Beyond J. Louis Martyn* (Eugene, OR: Cascade, 2012), 3.

4. Quoted in Collins, *Apocalyptic Imagination*, 1.

ery positive objectification of God."[5] Apocalyptic theology is today enjoying a renaissance, and for some of the same reasons. Apocalyptic disturbs settled opinion, resists fixities in all forms, demands existential response. The searing rhetoric of apocalyptic is ideally suited to a summons to the slumbering: "Wake up!"

Apocalyptic is no longer confined to the theologians. As Derrida said with characteristic playfulness, there is a "newly arisen apocalyptic tone in philosophy."[6] "The global capitalist system is approaching an apocalyptic zero-point," writes the anti-theologian Slavoj Zizek at the beginning of his *Living in the End Times*.[7] Four horsemen stalk the plains: "ecological crisis, the consequences of the biogenetic revolution, imbalances within the system itself . . . and the explosive growth of social divisions and exclusions."[8] Zizek means something analogous to the traditional understanding of apocalypse: Dreadful doom hangs over the world, and, as we shall see below, Zizek proposes an apocalyptically-infused response to the apocalypse.

---

5. Davis and Harink, *Apocalyptic and the Future of Theology,* 3.

6. Jacques Derrida, *Raising the Tone of Philosophy: Late Essays by Immanuel Kant, Transformative Critique by Jacques Derrida*, ed. Peter Fenves (Baltimore: Johns Hopkins University Press, 1993).

7. Slavoj Zizek, *Living in the End Times* (London: Verso, 2010), x.

8. Zizek, *Living in the End Times*, x.

In a related vein, Alain Badiou makes the quasi-apocalyptic "Event" the center of his philosophy. In a lecture, Badiou traces the sickness of contemporary philosophy, whether in its hermeneutic (Heidegger, Gadamer), its analytic (Wittgenstein and disciples), or its postmodern (you know who) guises, to two common flaws: all assume the end of metaphysics, which means the end of truth, and all assume that language is "the crucial site of thought." Badiou finds both of these assumptions disastrous. Philosophy is dead unless it can "establish itself beyond the multiplicity of language games."[9] Unless philosophy can affirm Truth, it has no way to stand against "the monetary uniformity imposed on us by global capitalism."

Truth cannot, however, be a traditionally transcendent truth communicated by revelation, nor can it be reliant on the foundational certainties of Cartesian modernity, nor the result of rigorous Kantian reasoning. Faith in truth cannot assume any unity in the universe. Instead, true philosophy must risk adhering to a "fixed point within discourse, a point of interruption," an event to which one remains absolutely loyal. Hence Badiou's interest in Paul, whom he considers "a poet-thinker of the event." Badiou has no interest or belief in the specifics of the gospel Paul preaches, but only in the formal structure of a Paul who announces

---

9. Frederiek Depoortere, *Badiou and Theology* (London: Bloomsbury, 2009).

a great event that defines truth in terms of faithfulness to the Event. Paul's letters "are in no way . . . narratives, in the manner of the Gospels, or theoretical treatises, of the kind later by the Church Fathers, or the lyrical prophecies, such as the Apocalypse attributed to John." No, "they are *interventions.*" Paul "propounds a speech of rupture, and writing ensues when necessary."[10]

Paul is the *anti*-philosopher, who resists every attempt to confine the gospel events into a system, most especially every attempt to manipulate the gospel to make it a form of Greek "wisdom" that draws its conclusions from the order of the cosmos, the way things always are. Nor can Paul be bundled together with the Jews, for whom signs play the role that wisdom plays in Greek philosophy. Jewish "discourse" is the discourse of the exception, "because the prophetic sign, the miracle, election, designate transcendence as that which lies behind the natural totality."[11] Neither wisdom nor signs define Paul's discourse. Following Paul's lead, one cannot start from the Whole or from the Exception; one can be neither Greek nor Jew but "must proceed from the event as such," which Badiou describes as "a-cosmic and illegal, refusing integration into any to-

---

10. Alain Badiou, *Saint Paul: The Foundation of Universalism* (Stanford: Stanford University Press, 2003), 31.

11. Badiou, *Saint Paul*, 41.

tality and signaling nothing."[12] For Paul, one event-complex, the incarnation, death, and resurrection of Jesus is the touchstone of everything, the touchstone of "physics" and "ethics."

Badiou clarifies by distinguishing discourses of the Father from those of the Son. Paternal discourses "bind communities in a form of obedience (to the Cosmos, the Empire, God, or the Law)." One (Greek) is a universalizing discourse of the Father; the other (Jewish) is a particular discourse of the Father. What is needed for what Badiou identifies as a true universal is a "discourse of the Son,"[13] a discourse that is "absolutely *new*," a discourse of rupture, mimicking God's sending of the Son that that constitutes and "signifies primarily an intervention within History." Through this intervention, Nietzsche says, history is "'broken in two,' rather than governed by a transcendental reckoning in conformity with the laws of an epoch. The sending (birth) of the son names this rupture. That it is the son, not the father, who is exemplary, enjoins us not to put our trust any longer in any discourse laying claim to the form of mastery."[14] Badiou's Event is a permanent apocalypse, a messianic advent that never arrives: "Christ is *a coming*; he

---

12. Badiou, *Saint Paul*, 4.

13. Badiou, *Saint Paul*, 42.

14. Badiou, *Saint Paul*, 43.

is what interrupts the previous regime of discourses, Christ is, in himself and for himself, *what happens to us.*"[15]

Badiou's philosophy has affinities with the apocalyptic outlook of other thinkers, but his understanding of the Event is more focused and personal. Badiou's own Damascus Road is less transcendent than Paul's: It is the revolt of May 1968. That political and cultural upheaval became the defining moment of Badiou's life. A philosophy loyal to the Event is characterized by revolt, logic, universality, and risk—all the features of genuine philosophy. In Badiou, May 1968 fits into the slot occupied by Christ's death and resurrection in Paul's theology. May 1968 is the Event to which Badiou declares his loyalty, the eruption that paradoxically gives stability and direction to life.

Badiou's Event philosophy has affinities with the work of Derrida and Walter Benjamin. Derrida reflects that the apocalyptic command to "Come," which calls the event that is yet to come, cannot be encompassed with any logic, including the "onto-theo-eschatology" of the event. Derrida has himself been read as an apocalyptic philosopher, and he admits that apocalyptic discourse has the capacity to elude censors and to "dismantle the dominant contract or concordat."[16] Yet the apocalyptic does not disclose an actual end. Were the advent to arrive, it would mean a closure

---

15. Badiou, *Saint Paul*, 48.

16. Badiou, *Saint Paul*, 160.

that would violate apocalyptic discourse itself. What apocalypse finally reveals, he suggests, is the demystification of apocalyptic itself. What is announced is "an apocalypse without apocalypse, an apocalypse without vision, without truth, without revelation."[17] Likewise, despite Benjamin's debt to Kabbalic sources, he has no interest in their interpretive practices or their texts. What he takes from Kabbalah is the sheerly formal reality of the "lightning flash" of a messianic moment, which has the advantage of disrupting and subverting all pretenses of utopia.[18]

For Badiou and the rest, though, the Event is only identifiable as such against the background of non-eventful reality. Events disrupt fixity, permanence, stability, stasis. Eruptions bubble up from a smooth and placid surface. But if all is multiplicity all the way down, how does one account for that fixity, or even the appearance of fixity? If all is multiplicity, so that it is really impossible to speak of "all" at all, it would seem that all is also event. But if that is the case, the Event cannot stand free of its context to compel adherence and loyalty. There is also the problem of judgment. After all, Heidegger (for some time at least) considered Hitler an *Ereignis* in very much the sense that Badiou means. More practically, or aesthetically, the spectacle of a

---

17. Derrida, *Raising the Tone*, 167.

18. Cyril O'Regan, *Theology and the Spaces of Apocalyptic* (Milwaukee: Marquette University Press, 2009), 61-68.

now-elderly French academic (Badiou was born in 1937) adhering gamely to 1968 is not a little embarrassing. The *Guardian* reporter who interviewed Badiou in May 2012 noticed the gleam that came to his eyes as he spoke of his life between 1968-1980, "as if he's recalling an old love affair he can never forget."[19]

This sketch isolates some of the problems in recent treatments of apocalyptic, and points to ways in which the work of Rosenstock-Huessy contributes to contemporary thought. Rosenstock-Huessy is as much a thinker of the Event as Badiou, but he is able to explain how Eventful disruptions leave their mark in ordinary life. He radicalizes and universalizes Event, but is able to give a compelling account of the Eventfulness of the everyday.

The following pages are mostly expositional, but within the exposition is an implied explanation of Rosenstock-Huessy's extraordinary version of the apocalyptic explanation. It is due to two basic and related features of all his work: His historical concreteness on the one hand, and his Christian orthodoxy on the other. He is able to navigate the issues of eruption and stasis because his thought is infused with the particularity of the incarnation, death, and resurrection of Jesus.

---

19. Stuart Jeffries, "Alain Badiou: A Life in Writing," 2012. www. theguardian.com/culture/2012/may/18/alain-badiou-life-in-writing.

I. Calendars and Revolution

Liberal Christianity dispensed with the primitive apoca-
lypticism that confesses a real end of the world, but for
Rosenstock-Huessy, the central affirmation of the creed is
that "Christians believe in an end of the world, *not only
once but again and again.*"[20] This is not simply a statement
about repeated catastrophes, but a confession of faith in
the intervention of Last Judgment into history. For Rosenstock-Huessy, past faith in a final future judgment was of
the essence of Christian faith and the motor of Christian
energy. If there is a final judgment, then there is *a* trajectory
to history, as it moves from the Alpha of creation toward
the Omega point of the unity of the human race. These
twin dimensions of judgment—the reality of real endings
in the middle of history and the movement toward a final
accounting—were essential to the Christian understanding
of progress in history. Without a real final judgment, history is headed nowhere; without apocalypses in the midst of
time, events simply accumulate one after the other, leaving
no way to discern the beginnings and endings of epochs.
Christian faith in a final judgment thus gave the world a
vision of a unified history. As that faith withers under the
influence of liberal theology, the West is left only with a
vision of "progresses," technical improvements in the absence of hope for the progress of humanity as such. Rosen-

---

20. *CF*, 61-61; emphasis added.

stock-Huessy sees this failure of faith in the abandonment of the Christian division of time into BC and AD, which "signifies the capitulation of theology before 'science'" and is "part of the suicide of Europe."[21]

Against this Christian creedal background, Rosenstock-Huessy tells the story of Western history and the Christian church as a series of "apocalypses," eruptive revolutions that remake time, language, and human experience. Revolution is not an odd anomaly in political history. Rather, "there is no Christian country and no national character which can boast that it is founded on evolutionary institutions alone."[22] Again and again, Rosenstock-Huessy says, the church has been dead, but it has always risen again, often with more brilliance than before. Out of the carnage of the church's bloodletting, she has produced a Dante, a More, a Luther.[23] Apocalypse settles out in the church's "risen" life.

The Western revolution most closely connected with Christian eschatology is the Papal Revolution of Gregory VII, which Rosenstock-Huessy describes as the first total revolution. At its heart, the Papal revolution was mutiny

---

21. *CF*, 73n5.

22. Quoted in Wayne Cristaudo, *Religion, Redemption, and Revolution: The New Speech Thinking of Franz Rosenzweig and Eugen Rosenstock-Huessy* (Toronto: University of Toronto Press, 2012), 250.

23. Cristaudo, *Religion, Redemption, and Revolution*, 209.

against the papacy's reliance on the palace: "The papacy cut the direct and domestic relation between throne and altar in every manor or palace, and claimed the right to be guardian and spokesman for every local representative of the spirit." The key issue was the election of the Pope, and "what the reform party did tackle immediately was the exclusion of the Roman nobility from the election of the pope." Behind this severance of the palace from the Papacy was the papal obsession with the *orb*, the world. Popes announced their decisions *urbi et orbi*, as the *urbs* came to contain the entire *orbis*. This vision of a universal city had a direct political effect in the Crusades, when the Pope was able to go over the heads of the various political rulers to summon troops to battle. "By summoning the Christians to Jerusalem, the papacy resuscitated the maritime character of the old Roman Empire." In all these ways, the Pope functioned as the "true emperor" of Europe.[24]

Popes saw this as a revival of Pauline spirit. Though claiming to be successors of Peter, Paul was invoked because of his universality, a view expressed in Peter Damian's remark that Paul "is the right arm of God, held out over the whole breadth of the earth, presiding over all churches."[25] Paul was also called upon to support the doctrine of two swords; as a Benjamite, he was associated with spiritual and

---

24. Rosenstock-Huessy, *Out of Revolution*, 533.

25. *Out of Revolution*, 534.

temporal authority. Thus, the new papal power was defended by appeals to both Peter and Paul: "The symbol of St. Paul, now reclaimed from the emperor, ceased to lead the unorganized movements in the Church against the established order. This prophetic function was forgotten for four hundred years, until it was re-invoked by Luther." When later medievals attacked the Papacy, they did it in the name of John, and hoped not for a Pauline but for a Johannine age to dawn.[26]

This medieval revolution was intertwined with the apocalyptic poetry of Dante's *Commedia*, which for the first time united planetary revolutions with human history by making the "revolutions of the stars the symbols of life, and their motivation identical with the passions of our own life."[27] Dante also gave expression to the imperial ideology of the time, according to which the emperor's interventions and judgments functioned as a foretaste of the final divine Judge. As he campaigned through Europe, "in Italy, in Poland, in France, in Burgundy, in Hungary, the emperor protected widows and orphans, the poor and the weak, against the local politician." The least serf could appeal over the head of the lord of the manor to the emperor's court, thus putting the emperor "in judgment over the wickedness of local despots" as a "legal vicar of the terrors

---

26. *Out of Revolution*, 535.

27. *Out of Revolution*, 500.

of the Last Judgment."[28] The Last Judgment also supported a unified vision of Europe as a single world. As the final judgment transcended all local and partial judgments, and so unified and equalized humanity, so the emperor's court transcended local powers and unified the peoples of Europe in a new Christian Roman empire. Rosenstock-Huessy provocatively suggests that "the Empire . . . was a Christian democracy."[29]

The greatest contribution of the Last Judgment to the medieval revolution came through the insertion of All Souls into the Christian calendar. Through the celebration of All Souls, the church "established the solidarity of all souls from the beginning of the world to the end of time."[30] It was truly the democracy of the dead, an embrace of death's role as the great equalizer into the heart of Christian civilization, and in this way "revealed man's dignity, his claim not to be thrown into the fire like a weed, but to be judged."[31] Consistent with the universal vision of All Souls, Odilo of Cluny initiated universal prayers in his monasteries: "Up to that time, monks had prayed only for their abbey, their relatives, their friends, their connections."[32]

---

28. *Out of Revolution*, 502.

29. *Out of Revolution*, 507.

30. *Out of Revolution*, 507.

31. *Out of Revolution*, 509.

32. *Out of Revolution*, 509.

All Souls was a decree of emancipation because it incorporated the reality of death into the rhythm of life, a calendrical embodiment of the gospel of the resurrection of the dead. For Rosenstock-Huessy, apocalyptic eruption of speech forms, molds, and articulates history.[33] Past and future are divided from each other by events and, importantly, our talk about events. The present becomes something more than the knife-edge of the passing moment because our speech and our listening create "bodies of time" with discernible beginnings and endings—the time of the play, the time of the game, the age of Victoria. Time is humanized, and it is no longer simply natural passage and movement, nor simply the dead time of the clock of physics, but historical time. These articulations of time are determined by human action. Humans act in revolutionary ways, and these revolutionary disruptions settle into a new social world through the human power to pronounce dead what is dead and to speak new things into being. Everything depends on getting the timing right. Rotten societies cannot be, and ought not be, propped up. Rosenstock-Huessy is on the side of the revolutionaries. But the dead must be pronounced dead at the right time. Too early or too late, a

---

33. See Peter J. Leithart, "The Social Articulation of Time in Eugen Rosenstock-Huessy," in *Modern Theology* 26 (Hoboken, NJ: Wiley, 2010), 197-219.

death certificate multiplies violence and needless destruction.[34]

Humanized time becomes culturally embodied in calendars, which mark out the normal time of a civilization. Calendars reveal history as the "autobiography" of a race, ultimately the unified autobiography of the entire human race. Rosenstock-Huessy notes at the beginning of *Out of Revolution* that mankind would lack autobiography if human society had "always been like modern society: completely sensational, totally forgetful, and wonderfully devoid of memory." But humanity has not always been so: "mankind has always, with the utmost tenacity, cultivated its calendar," and this is in itself a cultivation of memory.

> A day introduced into the calendar or a day stricken out of the calendar, means a real change in the education and tradition of a nation. Mankind writes its own history long before the historians visit its battlefields; days, festivals, holidays, the order of meals, rest and vacations, together with religiously observed rituals and symbols, are sources of political history, though rarely used by the average political or economic historian.[35]

---

34. Cristaudo, *Religion, Redemption, and Revolution*, 245.

35. *Out of Revolution*, 8.

Rosenstock-Huessy details many examples of how revolutions marked the calendar, articulated the Western past,
and shaped its historical memory, but I will limit myself
to one illustration, the Soviet calendar. In 1918, the Revolutionaries adopted the Gregorian calendar, synchronizing
Russian time with the time of the West. At the same time,
"local authorities began to emulate the French Revolution
by altering the names of the months and days, substituting
the names of old peasant leaders for Easter and Christmas,
for example." The national government suppressed these
local innovations, but also began a variety of calendrical
forms. In 1929, they introduced a five-day week, and abol-
ished the common day of rest. One effect was to undermine family and religious life: "A man and a wife would
never have the same day off unless they were in the same
'labour calendar.' In a family of more working individuals it became still more difficult to synchronize the leisure
time. Consequently, family ties were broken up as much as
religion."[36]

A common day of rest was re-introduced in 1932, and
by 1936 the Revolution had introduced a thorough revi-
sion of the calendar:

Whereas the year of 365 days remains divided into
twelve months, two parallel weeks have been in-

---

36. *Out of Revolution*, 121.

troduced, one of seven, and the other of six days. Labour, ministry and rest are to be regulated by the shorter, government and international intercourse by the longer. The rest days of the labour week fall on the sixth, twelfth, eighteen, twenty-fourth and thirtieth day of each month, with March 1 taking the place of the fifth rest day of February.[37]

Extra holidays were fixed—five in the first order, ten or twelve of second-order—far fewer than the pre-Revolutionary calendar based on inherited from the Orthodox church. Lenin Day is celebrated on January 22, and the minor holidays celebrate "Youth, Women, Sports, Anti-War": "A new polytheism of group ideals is established. Great powers and principalities: Labour, Youth, Womanhood, Peace sway this world in endless recurrence."[38]

In this discussion, Rosenstock-Huessy shows in concrete detail how the Event of the Russian Revolution becomes incorporated into the life of Russia through the calendar. Though the calendar signifies the "stasis" of time and is a marker of "normal time," it is *constituted* by disruptions. Without revolution, the calendar would have no shape; "normal" time would be un-articulated, truly inarticulate. The calendar is a mechanism for inserting apoc-

---

37. *Out of Revolution*, 121-2.

38. *Out of Revolution*, 122.

alyptic events into the rhythms of society, for taking up death into daily life.

II. Event in Everyday

In contrast to Badiou and Benjamin, Rosenstock-Huessy sees the world as an inherently tumultuous place and life as inherently distended, stretched, torn, and broken. History is not a darkness punctuated by a few bursts of light. Rosenstock-Huessy radicalizes Eventfulness to highlight how surprise, rupture, breach, and eruption are daily occurrences. More theologically, for Rosenstock-Huessy the apocalypse of the cross is not an occasional occurrence, but the very stuff of human life. We live in agony on the cross, pulled and torn at every moment, and yet at any moment we may also share in resurrection. Death and resurrection is not a rupture in a smooth surface of normalcy. Like Zizek, Rosenstock-Huessy says that the surface is a rupture, but he is able to show far more fully than Zizek the daily disruptions of death and renewal. Rosenstock-Huessy encompasses both large-scale apocalypse—the end of a world and the beginning of a new—and the liveliness of everyday life in a single framework, centered on the cross.

Everyday Eventfulness comes into particular focus in Rosenstock-Huessy's treatment of language. He is scornful of language philosophy for abstracting language from the situations in which humans speak and write. "For Wittgenstein," he writes, "philosophy is no more and no less than the analysis of statements in terms of other statements; what a living person does or should do about any state is not the province of philosophy." Wittgenstein, Russell and the rest ignore the *reality* of words and symbols, and their "active and activating power" that not only comes from but can "even make human history." For all their logic, language philosophers remain human beings, a fact evident when they respond in anger to the charge that they are illogical and unreasonable: That is, they "respond illogically and unreasonably to at least the 'sacred names' of Logic and Reason."[39] Philosophy in general has "unphilosophical," existential roots. Notable philosophers from Paracelsus to Descartes all the way to Nietzsche are "sons of the catastrophes through which they suffered." When other philosophers suffer other catastrophes, their suffering will squeeze out something else; prior philosophy must be "changed, must be lived down."[40] Language philosophy tries to suppress the Events that force speech from us. The bias of linguistics against rupture runs deep. Rosenstock-Huessy spots an error in the basic assumption that language is a tool of the mind, used primarily to express thought. That theory is understandable coming from comfortable tenured professors, but in reality speech is a bid to overcome

---

39. Quoted in Cristaudo, *Religion, Redemption, and Revolution*, 69.

40. Quoted in Cristaudo, *Religion, Redemption, and Revolution*, 75.

death or to "enhance the love that has befallen us."[41] Speech does not mainly function to communicate thought, but to awaken us from slumber.[42]

Positively, Rosenstock-Huessy's grammatical sociology highlights the very features of language that language philosophy ignores. The dogmas of grammar are the final bastion of antiquity: "The schools have shelved Euclidean geometry, Ptolemaic astronomy, Galenian medicine, Roman law and Christian dogma," but cling to "ancient grammatical dogma."[43] The problem with the "Alexandrian table of grammar" that every beginning Latin student employs (*amo, amas, amat*, etc.) is that "all persons are put through the same drill. They all seem to speak in the same manner." On the Alexandrian system, "all these sentences can and should be treated as of the same social character."[44] The texture of speech is smoothed over in what Rosenstock-Huessy describes as a "fatal error,"[45] because "*amo* and *amas* are treated as though they too were mere statements of fact as *amat*."[46]

---

41. Quoted in Cristaudo, *Religion, Redemption, and Revolution*, 79, 81.

42. Cristaudo, *Religion, Redemption, and Revolution*, 87.

43. *Speech and Reality*, 98.

44. *SR*, 100.

45. *SR*, 100.

46. *SR*, 108.

Existentially, grammatical persons are not on a par. We utter "*amat*" or "*amatur*" without any stake in the sentence we utter. The distancing third person can be uttered only by someone on the outside of the relationship of love, only by someone for whom the love spoken of is powerless. Third-person talk of God has the same effect: "God in prayer, God in the ten commandments—is the living God. God as the object of theology is powerless, a mere third person." The negation of the third person is a double-negation, not only abstracting the speaker from his speech but from the listener as well. Bill and Ted might debate the truth of *amat* concerning Al, but the outcome of the debate is indifferent to Bill and Ted. Only when we recognize this double negation can we see "the abyss between the objective third person in *amat* and the two conversing people who exchange their views about him as subject and preject."[47]

If *amat* represents stasis, the first person represents a moment of rupture. *Amat* implies no commitment from either the speaking subject or the hearing preject, but *amo* is risky business. To speak *amo* is to admit I am involved in the act of which we speak. I cannot say *amo* detachedly, without self-commitment; if I do, I am guilty of deception. Anyone who says *amo* "runs a risk which he does not run in speaking of somebody else! He runs the risk of destroying

---

47. *SR*, 100-2.

the act to which the sentence testifies."[48] As every Shakespearean romantic comedy shows, a man who says *amo* risks interference—from a rival, from parents, from the law.[49] *Amo* is socially disruptive in a way that *amat* is not. A report that says "amat" doesn't change anything; it conservatively describes what is already the case. But "the speaker of a sentence in the first person cannot help changing his own social situation simply by divulging any act, thought, feeling, intention of himself."[50] Because of the risks, *amo* tends to be uttered in the safety of a private space: "To the world, if I am intelligent at all, I shall not say *amo* but *uxor mea est*. That is, I shall transform the first person sentence into a third person sentence," since the latter does not invite interference, rivalry, jealousy, wrath.[51]

To utter the *first* person, one must break through a natural reluctance to express what is within. To utter a *second* person sentence, we have to break through the reluctance of a hearer to hear. To speak a sentence in the second person is always to assume an office; there is an implicit hierarchy in every "you." Even if the statement is simply "you have bad breath," it assumes that the speaker has some authority to speak, or it will be greeted with a response

---

48. *SR*, 102.

49. *SR*, 103.

50. *SR*, 103.

51. *SR*, 104.

ranging between indifference and a punch in the snoot: "Why is advice unasked for never given successfully? Because it has no power to unlock the recipient's ear."[52] To utter a second-person sentence, we have to convert the hearer into a listener.[53] In sum,

> the speaker of *amo* has made up his mind to break his silence about himself although this means running the risk of intervention. The listener of *amas* has made up his mind to invite interference. The speaker and listener of *amat* have nothing to readjust in their own political attitude before they listen to this fact. They are neither defying nor inviting interference in their own affairs.[54]

Amo and *amas* disrupt not only the life of the speaker but that of the listener. Robert Jenson has made the Rosenstockian observation that every utterance breaks into the listener's world and opens up fresh possibility for the future. If I say "*I* love you," I forcibly present some options to the hearer—to respond in kind, to recoil, to draw near or to flee. A personal address is always an implicit second-person; despite its strict grammatical form "Good morning"

---

52. *SR*, 106.

53. *SR*, 106.

54. *SR*, 106.

is not an indicative statement about the weather but an invitation to conversation. Like *amo*, it breaks into the life of the hearer and forces him or her to choose a future—to smile, to extend the conversation, to look desperately for another seat on the bus.[55]

Whoever speaks kills and makes alive.[56] We miss this power of language because we learn grammar in a form that already embodies the Cartesian primacy of the Ego, a grammar that makes the "I" the "first person." On the contrary, Rosenstock-Huessy insists, "all our experience teaches us exactly the opposite of this Greek premise, that the single 'I' is primary." A child develops by "gradually stak[ing] out its borders as an independent entity," by si-phoning out the "thousand cares, impressions, and influences which surround, flow around, and beset it." What a child first recognizes is not a world, nor father and mother, but "that it is spoken to": "It is smiled at, entreated, rocked, comforted, punished, given presents, or nourished. It is first a 'you' to a powerful being outside itself—above all to its parents."[57] Goethe said that a father is always his daughter's first god. Rosenstock-Huessy agrees, adding that "He is so because he is present for his daughter before her own 'I' is,

---

55. Jenson, *Essays in Theology of Culture.*

56. Rosenstock-Huessy, *Die Sprache des Menschengeschlects,* 1.143; "Wer spricht, toten und macht lebendig."

57. Rosenstock-Huessy, "Practical Knowledge of the Soul," 16.

and because he bestows on her the consciousness of herself, by addressing her as 'you.'"[58] Rupture is not a break in the social foundation. Small-scale ruptures happen all the time, in second-person address, imperatives, in first-person self-expressions. Rupture is foundational. Epoch-making apocalyptic events echo in the Event of daily speech.

Not all social relations, not all speech situations, not all forms of silence, are the same. When two or three are gathered, they may possess a single spirit of unanimity, they may split, they may be cautious, and the may be strangers. In the first case, speaker and listener already share one spirit as members of the same "in-group." When two meet as strangers, they are "outside" one another, with no common spirit and no common language, and the mode of speech and listening is different. Speech situations may involve old and young, as the old utter sacramental words to be repeated by the young; or friends in agreement, so that their relation is like a soloist and a chorus; strangers are people in disagreement, and depend on question and answer; and leader and led are in a command and response relationship.[59] In sum,

> Magister and disciple, singer and chorus, leader
> and respondent are of equal originality in their lin-

---

58. *PKS*, 16.

59. *SR*, 124.

guistic situation as the interlocutors of a discussion in the form of question and answer. By isolating the interrogatory mood, the origin of question and answer was inexplicable until today. As soon as we compare the prosaic process of question and answer to its parallels in historical tradition (formula and repetition), in musical unanimity (singer and chorus), in political challenge (imperative and response), question and answer are disclosed as one application of the general principle of social relations to be established through speech, the application to the meeting of two people from different spaces, and therefore of a different standard of objectivity.[60]

One of the themes highlighted in this paragraph is the centrality of imperatives. Contrary to modern prejudice, imperatives are emancipating, not confining. "Love God and your neighbor as yourself" are the most freeing words ever spoken. A command cuts through the confusion and paralysis of indecision and forces us to action. We act only if we are "able to hear without [ourselves] the clear-cut alternative: shall I do this, or not do this?" The "disease of our time" is a problem of "conflicting suggestions in great number," and only an authoritative "Do this" cuts through

---

60. *SR*, 126.

and leads to action. The fundamental imperative, however, is the imperative "Listen" or "Be interested." This is not only the general imperative behind all other imperatives, but it is the imperative behind all other forms of speech. The scientist carries out his objective science in response to a summons, "Let there be science!" Rosenstock-Huessy illustrates the more general point by thinking through the phrase "The darkened moon." This may be a piece of lyrical speech, part of a poem; it might be a narrative, part of a story; it could be a phrase from a scientific treatise. But behind all these is the imperative: "Look, the darkened moon." Each of these is intonated differently: The poetic speech is rhythmical and emotional, the factual definition is pronounced with accent, the story aims at propriety. But these all depend on an emphatic statement, "Look! A Darkened Moon! Pay attention! Listen! Hear!" If there is an implied imperative in every utterance, there is likewise a possibility for "apocalyptic" intervention every time we speak and listen. Every conversation is potentially life-changing. Every time we open our mouths, we may end an era and begin a new one, both for ourselves and for our hearers.

In Rosenstock-Huessy's grammatical sociology, in short, *everyday* language is Eventful speech. Imperatives, names, direct second-person address, first-person revelations are the stuff of social interaction, and each of them would be a rupture in the fabric, did the fabric exist at all. For Rosenstock-Huessy, the fabric is itself constituted by rupture. Certain events loom larger than others, but event-fulness is the ordinary course of life.

III. Conclusion

Rosenstock-Huessy's emphasis on the Eventfulness of the everyday and his sensitivity to the apocalyptic shape of history enables him to incorporate the best insights of the postmodern thinkers with whom we began, and to transcend them. He subsumes both apocalypse and philosophies of the Event in a larger outlook, the Cross of Reality. From Rosenstock-Huessy's perspective, Derrida is right to insist that apocalypse is a "transcendental" mode of speech, right to see it in the imperative "Come."[61] To that insight, however, Rosenstock-Huessy adds rich and concrete detail, both with regard to everyday uses of language and with regard to the apocalyptic impact of historical events. Within his framework, Rosenstock-Huessy can include the kind of life-forming event that Badiou describes. Each day's imperatives and addresses confront speakers and listeners with the possibility of a fresh path into the future, but Rosenstock-Huessy recognizes that specific events may decisively shape an individual's life. For Rosenstock-Huessy, the Event of all events was World War I, a truly epoch-shattered, apocalyptic event in history that sent its aftershocks into Rosenstock-Huessy through the remainder of his life.

---

61. Derrida, *Raising the Tone*, 156-7.

Rosenstock-Huessy transcends contemporary thinkers of apocalypse, however, because he maintains connections between apocalyptic or eschatology in the normal Christian sense and the everyday Eventfulness that I have described. The cross and resurrection of Jesus, and the promise of final judgment, lie at the heart of his understanding of Eventfulness, both in everyday life and in larger historical movements.

Rosenstock-Huessy's description of language provides the best evidence of the theological ground of his philosophy of Eventfulness. Speech removes the skin that separates human beings and unites together in a single complex action, and for Rosenstock-Huessy this dynamic articulates time into "bodies" with distinct beginnings and endings. An order given by one person initiates a series of actions by those who are under his orders; but the action is not done until it is reported back—not in an imperative but in an indicative. The order-and-report sequence creates "one common time" between the commander and the one obeying the order, a "supertime" that "neglects the separation of two bodies and their biological times." Speech creates a single time. This is not accurately described as a "common frame of reference" since a "'frame' seems to exist outside our sayings or acts." It is rather a "field of correspondence" that "breaks down the separation of two 'self-contained' bodies; it gets 'under the skin,' and they act as a single will from the moment the order is given to the moment it is reported fulfilled. After this, the field collapses and disappears."[62] Time in daily experience as in historical events is articulated, textured, given its specific contours by our speech.

Speech has this time-shaping power because it has the capacity to declare beginnings and endings. The past is not past until we pronounce it so; the dead must be certified as dead; the dead must be buried with fitting rites and words. Rosenstock-Huessy provides a concrete illustration: "As long as people have not *said so*, they may sleep, eat, work together, and yet not be married at all." Until they pronounce the "I do" of their wedding vows, they have not closed off their bachelor options.[63] For Rosenstock-Huessy, only this distinguishes a Christian view of time from pagan cyclicism: "the cycle is an eternal myth at which we stare," while Christian progress arises from "an act of our own creative faith," an act that simultaneously declares what is dead and opens a pathway to the future.[64]

Rosenstock-Huessy links this power of speech to the Christian gospel, which, he claims, is fundamentally an eschatological announcement. Paganism resisted death, and creatively constructed mechanisms of death avoidance. Christianity embraces the reality of death in life, and turns

---

62. Rosenstock-Huessy, *Origin of Speech*, 47.

63. *CF*, 79.

64. *CF*, 79.

the old common sense on its head: Instead of accepting that life leads to death, Christianity claimed that death opens up life, and thereby made it possible for human beings to re-enact the death and resurrection of Jesus over and over within history. Jesus was the first to live *"from the end of time* back into his own age,"[65] since by the resurrection He lives on the far side of death. Christians follow Jesus in putting to death their old selves, their old loyalties, allegiances, social networks, confident of a life beyond that grave. In this way, humanity "has acquired partnership in God's deepest wisdom, when to let go, when to say farewell, when to end a chapter of evolution."[66] It is the wisdom to *end*, to declare the dead to be dead, without being paralyzed by the fear of death but instead being buoyed by the confidence of new life. Christianity and future are synonymous,[67] but that is only because the "last judgment" and the "end of the world" have been embraced in the middle of history, only because of the incorporation of apocalyptic endings and new beginnings into daily experience.

By the same token, Rosenstock-Huessy's biblical conception of creation *ex nihilo* also supports an apocalyptic outlook. In ancient mythologies and philosophies, the cosmos takes shape from a formless but somehow-ex-

---

65. *CF*, 67.

66. *CF*, 68.

67. *CF*, 62.

isting prime matter. That matter may be chaotic, but it provides a background for the emergence of an ordered world. For Christianity, though, creation is itself eruption, a bringing-into-being of something when there was nothing. There is no pre-existing surface to disrupt. Creation is sheer disruption, and new creation is a volcano in the midst of the upheavals of history, a volcano that gives birth to more, to *recurring*, fresh upheavals. Rosenstock-Huessy is thus able to sustain his vision of everyday Eventfulness—of moment-by-moment disruption, challenge, break, new paths—and of apocalypse—of dramatic epoch-forming upheavals—only because of his commitment to Christian faith.

BIBLIOGRAPHY

Adam, Barbara. "Social Versus Natural Time: A Traditional Distinction Re-Examined." In *The Rhythms of Society*. Edited by Michael Young and Thomas Schuller. London: Routledge, 1988.

Adam, Barbara. *Time*. Cambridge: Polity Press, 2004.

Adam, Barbara. *Time and Social Theory*. Philadelphia: Temple University Press, 1990.

Badiou, Alain. *Saint Paul: The Foundation of Universalism*. Stanford: Stanford University Press, 2003.

Barth, Karl. *Church Dogmatics*, I/2. Edinburgh: T&T Clark, 2004.

Begbie, Jeremy. *Theology, Music and Time*. Cambridge: Cambridge University Press, 2000.

Berman, Harold. *Law and Revolution: The Formation of the Western Legal Tradition*. Cambridge, Mass: Harvard University Press, 1983.

Betz, John R. "Enlightenment Revisited: Hamann as the First and Best Critic of Kant's Philosophy." In *Modern Theology* 20, 291-301. Hoboken, NJ: Wiley, 2004.

Betz, John R. "Hamann's London Writings: The Hermeneutics of Trinitarian Condescension." In *Pro Ecclesia* 14, 191-234. Dillsburg, PA: Center for Catholic and Evangelical Theology, 2005.

Blatnitzky, Leora. "Dialogue as Judgment, not Mutual Affirmation: A New Look at Franz Rosenzweig's Dialogic Philosophy." In *Journal of Religion* 79:4, 523-44. Chicago, IL: University of Chicago Press, 1999.

Braitermen, Zachary. "'Into Life'??! Franz Rosenzweig and the Figure of Death." In *AJS Review*, 23:2, 203-21. Philadelphia, PA: University of Pennsylvania Press, 1998.

Bryant, M. Darrol and Hans R. Huessy, eds. *Eugen Rosenstock-Huessy: Studies in His Life and Thought.* Lewiston, NY: Edwin Mellen Press, 1986.

Bryant, M. Darrol. "The Grammar of the Spirit: Time, Speech and Society." In *Eugen Rosenstock-Huessy: Studies in His Life and Thought.* Edited by M. Darrol Bryant and Hans R. Huessy. Lewiston, NY: Edwin Mellen, 1986.

Buchsel, Elfriede. "Das verlassiche Wort: Eugen Rosen-stock-Huessy und Johann Georg Hamann." In *Neue Zeitschrift fur systematische Theologie und Religionsphilosophie*, 42:1, 32-42. Berlin: Walter de Gruyter, 2000.

Busch, Eberhard. *The Great Passion: An Introduction to Karl Barth's Theology.* Translated by Geoffrey Bromiley. Grand Rapids, MI: Eerdmans, 2004.

Cohn, Norman. *The Pursuit of the Millennium: Revolutionary Millenarians and Mystical Anarchists of the Middle Ages.* Oxford: Oxford University Press, 1970.

Collins, John J. *The Apocalyptic Imagination: An Introduction to Jewish Apocalyptic Literature.* 2nd ed. Grand Rapids: Eerdmans, 1998.

Cristaudo, Wayne. *Religion, Redemption, and Revolution: The New Speech Thinking of Franz Rosenzweig and Eugen Rosenstock-Huessy.* Toronto: University of Toronto Press, 2012.

Cristaudo, Wayne. "Eugen Rosenstock-Huessy." In *Stanford Encyclopedia of Philosophy*, 2008. www.seop.leeds. uk/entries/rosenstock-huessy.

Davis, Joshua B. and Douglas Harink. *Apocalyptic and the Future of Theology: With and Beyond J. Louis Martyn.* Eugene, OR: Cascade, 2012.

Derrida, Jacques. *Raising the Tone of Philosophy: Late Essays by Immanuel Kant, Transformative Critique by Jacques Derrida*. Edited by Peter Fenves. Baltimore: Johns Hopkins University Press, 1993.

Depoortere, Frederiek. *Badiou and Theology*. London: Bloomsbury, 2009.

Elias, Norbert. *An Essay on Time*. Collected Works of Norbert Elias. Vol. 9. Dublin: University College Dublin Press, 1992.

Galli, Barbara, ed. *Cultural Writings of Franz Rosenzweig*. Library of Jewish Philosophy; Syracuse University Press, 2000.

Galli, Barbara. "Franz Rosenzweig and the name of God." In *Modern Judaism* 14:1, 63-86. Oxford: Oxford University Press, 1994.

Gibbs, Robert. *Correlations in Rosenzweig and Levinas*. Princeton: Princeton University Press, 1992.

Giddens, Anthony. *Central Problems in Social Theory: Action, Structure, and Contradiction in Social Analysis*. Berkeley: University of California Press, 1979.

Glatzer, Nahum. *Franz Rosenzweig: His Life and Thought*. 3rd ed. Indianapolis, IN: Hackett Publishing, 1998.

Gordon, Peter Eli. "Rosenzweig and Heidegger: Translation, Ontology, and the Anxiety of Affiliation." In *New German Critique* 77, 113-148. Durham, NC: Duke University Press, 1999.

Gower, Calvin W. "'Camp William James': A New Deal Blunder?" In *The New England Quarterly* 38:4. Cambridge, MA: MIT Press, 1965.

Gunton, Colin. *The One, the Three and the Many: God, Creation, and the Culture of Modernity.* Cambridge: Cambridge University Press, 1993.

Horton, Michael. *Covenant and Eschatology: The Divine Drama.* Louisville, KY: Westminster John Knox Press, 2002.

Jeffries, Stuart. "Alain Badiou: A Life in Writing." 2012. www.theguardian.com/culture/2012/may/18/alain-badiou-life-in-writing.

Jenson, Robert W. *Essays in Theology of Culture.* Grand Rapids, MI: Eerdmans, 1995.

Jenson, Robert W. "What Is the Point of Trinitarian Theology?" In *Trinitarian Theology Today: Essays on Divine Being and Act.* Edited by Christoph Schwobel. Edinburgh: T&T Clark, 1995.

Kepnes, Steven. "Rosenzweig's Liturgical Reasoning as Response to Augustine's Temporal Aporias." In *Liturgy, Time, and the Politics of Redemption*. Edited by Randi Rashkover and C. C. Pecknold. Radical Traditions. Grand Rapids, MI: Eerdmans, 2006.

Kern, Stephen. *The Culture of Time and Space*. 1983. Reprint, Cambridge: Harvard University Press, 2003.

Kerr, Fergus. *Theology After Wittgenstein*. Rev. ed. London: SPCK, 1997.

Knight, Douglas. *The Eschatological Economy: Time and the Hospitality of God*. Grand Rapids, MI: Eerdmans, 2006.

Knight, Douglas. "Jenson on Time." In *Trinity, Time, and Church: A Response to the Theology of Robert Jenson*. Edited by Colin Gunton. Grand Rapids, MI: Eerdmans, 2000.

Leithart, Peter J. "Speech on the Cross." In *The Cross and the Star*, edited by Wayne Cristaudo and Frances Huessy. Cambridge: Cambridge Scholars Press, 2009.

Leithart, Peter J. "The Social Articulation of Time in Eugen Rosenstock-Huessy." In *Modern Theology* 26, 197-219. Hoboken, NJ: Wiley, 2010.

Lindbeck, George. *The Nature of Doctrine: Religion and Theology in a Postliberal Age*. Louisville, KY: Westminster John Knox Press, 1984.

Milbank, John. "The Linguistic Turn as a Theological Turn." In *The Word Made Strange: Theology, Language, and Culture*. London: Blackwell, 1997.

Moltmann, Jurgen. *The Coming of God: Christian Eschatology*. Translated by Margaret Kohl. Minneapolis: Augsburg/Fortress, 2004.

Morgan, George Allen. *Speech and Society: The Christian Linguistic Social Philosophy of Eugen Rosenstock-Huessy*. Gainesville: University of Florida Press, 1987.

Mumford, Lewis. *The Human Prospect*. Boston: Beacon Press, 1955.

O'Malley, Michael. *Keeping Watch: A History of American Time*. New York: Penguin, 1990.

O'Regan, Cyril. *Theology and the Spaces of Apocalyptic*. Milwaukee: Marquette University Press, 2009.

Pickstock, Catherine. *After Writing: On the Liturgical Consummation of Philosophy*. Oxford: Blackwell, 1998.

Rashkover, Randi. *Revelation and Theopolitics: Barth, Rosenzweig and the Politics of Praise*. London: T&T Clark, 2005.

Rosenstock-Huessy, Eugen. *The Christian Future: Or the Modern Mind Outrun*. San Francisco: Harper, 1946.

Rosenstock-Huessy, Eugen. *Die Sprache des Menschengeschlects: Eine Leibhaftige Grammatik in Vier Teilen*. 2 vols. Heidelberg: Verlag Lambert Schneider, 1963.

Rosenstock-Huessy, Eugen. *The Fruit of Our Lips*. Eugene, OR: Wipf & Stock, 2021.

Rosenstock-Huessy, Eugen. *I Am An Impure Thinker*. Norwich, VT: Argo Books, 1970.

Rosenstock-Huessy, Eugen, ed. *Judaism Despite Christianity*. University of Alabama Press, 1969.

Rosenstock-Huessy, Eugen. *The Multiformity of Man*. Norwich, VT: Argo Books, 1973.

Rosenstock-Huessy, Eugen. *The Origin of Speech*. Norwich, VT: Argo Books, 1981.

Rosenstock-Huessy, Eugen. *Out of Revolution: Autobiography of Western Man*. London: Jarrolds Publishers, 1938.

Rosenstock-Huessy, Eugen. "Practical Knowledge of the Soul." Norwich, VT: Argo Books, 1988.

Rosenstock-Huessy, Eugen. *Speech and Reality*. Norwich, VT: Argo Books, 1970.

Rosenstock-Huessy, Eugen. "Man Must Teach." In *Rosenstock-Huessy Papers*. Vol. 1. Norwich, VT: Argo Books, 1940.

Rosenstock-Huessy, Eugen. "The Metabolism of Science." In *Rosenstock-Huessy Papers*. Vol. 1. Norwich, VT: Argo Books, 1981.

Rosenstock-Huessy, Eugen. "Time-Bettering Days." In *Rosenstock-Huessy Papers*. Vol. 1. Norwich, VT: Argo Books, 1954.

Rosenzweig, Franz. *Philosophical and Theological Writings*. Translated by Paul W. Franks and Michael L. Morgan. Indianapolis, IN: Hackett Publishing, 2000.

Rosenzweig, Franz. *Star of Redemption*. Translated by Barbara Galli. Madison, Wisconsin: University of Wisconsin Press, 2005.

Schmemann, Alexander. *For the Life of the World*. Crestwood, NY: St. Vladimir's Seminary Press, 1997.

Smith, James K. A. *The Fall of Interpretation: Philosophical Foundations for a Creational Hermeneutic.* Downers Grove: InterVarsity, 2000.

Smith, James K. A. *Speech and Theology: Language and the Logic of Incarnation.* London: Routledge, 2002.

Smith, James K. A. *Jacques Derrida: Live Theory.* New York: Continuum, 2005.

Stahmer, Harold M. "'Speech-Letters' and 'Speech-Thinking': Franz Rosenzweig and Eugen Rosenstock-Huessy." In *Modern Judaism* 4:1, 57-81. Oxford: Oxford University Press, 1984.

Stahmer, Harold. "Speak that I May See Thee!" In *The Religious Significance of Language.* New York: Macmillan, 1968.

Thiselton, Anthony. *Two Horizons.* Grand Rapids, MI: Eerdmans, 1980.

Thiselton, Anthony. *New Horizons in Hermeneutics.* Grand Rapids, MI: Zondervan, 1992.

Vanhoozer, Kevin. *The Drama of Doctrine: A Canonical-Linguistic Approach to Christian Theology.* Louisville, KY: Westminster John Knox Press, 2005.

Vanhoozer, Kevin. *First Theology: God, Scripture, and Hermeneutics*. Downers Grove: InterVarsity, 2002.

Vanhoozer, Kevin. *Is There a Meaning in this Text?* Grand Rapids, MI: Zondervan, 1998.

Von Balthasar, Hans Ur. *Theo-Drama: Theological Dramatic Theory, IV: The Action*. Translated by Graham Harrison. San Francisco, CA: Ignatius, 1994.

Zizek, Slavoj. *Living in the End Times*. London: Verso, 2010.

www.ingramcontent.com/pod-product-compliance
Lightning Source LLC
Chambersburg PA
CBHW071324120626
46546CB00002B/429